$17.95

Finally in print in a single volume, a selection
from Baraka's mostly out-of-print collections
of poetry, from 1961 to the present. Starting
with *Preface to a Twenty Volume Suicide Note*
and concluding with recent limited-edition
chapbooks and broadsides, this selection
traces the more than thirty year career of a
major writer who — along with Ezra Pound
— may be one of the most significant, and
least understood, American poets of our
century.

Edited by noted poet and translator Paul
Vangelisti, *Transbluesency* offers an ample
selection of works from every period of
Baraka's extraordinarily innovative, often
controversial struggle as a serious and
ideologically committed American artist —
from Beat to Black Nationalist to Marxist-
Leninist. This volume reveals a writer shaping
a body of poetry that is as well a body of
knowledge; a passionate reflection upon the
cultural, political, and aesthetic questions of
his time.

MARSILIO PUBLISHERS
Cover design: Looking
Photos: Charles Traub

TRANSBLUESENCY

The Selected Poems of
Amiri Baraka/LeRoi Jones
(1961–1995)

Edited by Paul Vangelisti

Marsilio Publishers
New York

CONTENTS

Black Magic (1969)

Hard Facts (1972)

FOREWORD

by Paul Vangelisti

This selection traces the almost forty-year career of a writer who, along with Ezra Pound, may be one of the most significant and least understood American poets of our century. *Transbluesency*[1] assembles the lifework, from the 1950s to the present, of a truly innovative figure: shaping a body of poetry that is as well a body of knowledge, a passionate, often self-critical reflection on the culture and politics of his time.

As he moves from so-called "Beat" to Nationalist to Third World Socialist, Baraka remains difficult to approach, particularly for a literary establishment positioned somewhere between Anglo-American academicism and the Entertainment industry. As the anthologist M.L. Rosenthal wrote, "No American poet since Pound has come closer to making poetry and politics reciprocal forms of action."[2] This came a decade after Rosenthal, in *The New Poets: American and British Poetry Since World War II*, had praised the early, ostensibly "Beat" poet as possessing "a natural gift for quick, vivid imagery and spontaneous humor."[3] For a critic like Rosenthal, grounded in the Cold War university aestheticism of the fifties, an apolitical bohemianism like the Beats,' keeping rebellion and art distinct from politics, would not necessarily be a threat. And, in the long run, such bohemianism would prove not unfriendly, perhaps even stimulating to the histories of established institutions. Instead, a politicized avant-garde like Baraka's, seeking an alternative form of aesthetic and social behavior, was and *is* clearly another matter.

[1] Both title and epigraph, "A blue fog you can almost see through," are from a Duke Ellington composition, on his 1946 Carnegie Hall LP.
[2] *Salmagundi*, nos. 22-23 (1973), quoted in *The LeRoi Jones/Amiri Baraka Reader*, p.xxi.
[3] Ibid., p. xix.

What distinguishes Baraka from the start is a kind of lyrical realism that sounds in counterpoint to his Beat contemporaries, steeped as they were in the egocentric idealism of nineteenth-century Anglo-American literature. Like Jack Spicer, Frank O'Hara, Paul Blackburn or Gilbert Sorrentino, *around* but not *of* the Beat public relations machinery, Baraka acknowledged a clear debt to the Anglo-American modernism of Pound and W.C. Williams, while seeking to develop other more international measures throughout his career. It is, in essence, the experimental, materialist, and anti-romantic overtones of the historical avant-gardes, as they filter through Pound and Williams, that place Baraka's poetry in an international twentieth-century tradition, which is both American (i.e., African-American, of the "New World") and firmly outside Anglo-American culture.

In 1912 (the year F.T. Marinetti, flying six hundred and fifty feet above the chimneys of Milan, heard the propeller speak the death of the psychological self and the birth of a lyric obsession with the physical), Ezra Pound wrote that he was in search of a more precise, active speech, a "language to think in."[4] Some fifty years later, after two world wars, and with imperial America clearly on the march, Baraka's first book, *Preface to a Twenty Volume Suicide Note*, underlines the urgency of a thoughtful, African-American poetic language. An early indication of this language's parameters is in "Hymn for Lanie Poo," fixing the historical ironies of the rebellious, colonial Rimbaud with the epigraph: "*Vous êtes des faux Négres.*" The "Hymn" finds its pulse in a parodic reliquary of the avant-garde "Saint"—who, having run off to Paris at age sixteen, clamored, in a notorious letter to his high school literature teacher, about the primal, "universal poetry" of mind and soul.[5] Baraka's young minstrel/bard ("*schwartze bohemien*" as he refers to himself and friends) opens his mock ode to the primordial in a self-conscious slapstick, playing both within and without his subject:

[4] Marinetti's "Technical Manifesto of Futurist Literature," from *Let's Murder the Moonshine: Selected Writings*, Los Angeles: Sun&Moon Press, 1991, p. 92; Pound's "A Retrospect," from *Literary Essays*, New York: New Directions, 1968, pp. 3-4.
[5] Rimbaud, *Complete Works*, Wallace Fowlie ed. & trans., U. of Chicago Press, 1966, p. 304.

O,
these wild trees
will make charming wicker baskets,
the young woman
the young black woman
the young black beautiful woman
said.

    These wild-assed trees
    will make charming
    wicker baskets.

(now, I'm putting words in her mouth . . . tch).

In "Way Out West" (after Sonny Rollins's title composition from the 1957 Los Angeles LP), Baraka improvises upon and ultimately re-evaluates that other great Anglo-American figure, T.S. Eliot, and his monumental rhetorical powers. In the infinitude of empty Western space, the eyes of Prufrock's dream melody are made to open wide, to be shut with a certain finality at song's end:

No use for beauty
collapsed, with moldy breath
done in. Insidious weight
of cankered dreams. Tiresias'
weathered cock.

Walking into the sea, shells
caught in the hair. Coarse
waves tearing the tongue.

Closing the eyes. As
simple an act. You float

Topography becomes even more extremely and self-consciously defined in the collage piece "Vice." Here Baraka introduces the theme of rage in exile, from a language and culture where the poem seems an incessant reminder of a distance still to be travelled, a music still to be formed:

This is *not* rage. (I am not that beautiful!) Only immobile coughs
& gestures towards somethings I don't understand. If I were lucky
enough to still be an adolescent, I'd just attribute these weird
singings in my intestine to sex, & slink off merrily to mastur
bate. Mosaic of disorder I own but cannot recognize. Mist in me.

In the sparse and intimate lyric of "Betancourt" (dated "30 July 1960 / Habana":
the poet's pivotal visit to Cuba Libre), the exiled rage and distance is, for the
moment, reversed. Baraka doesn't look out at the world from inside the poem's
North American boundaries, but rather from "some / new greenness," sur-
rounded by a braver language, where "flame / is the mind / . . . on strange
islands of warmth." He does in that exquisite instance gaze back, from outside,
from a revolutionary island and distance, toward poem and country:

> (I mean I think
> I know now
> what a poem
> is) A
> turning away . . .
> from what
> it was
> had moved
> us . . .
>   A .
> madness.

Back home in the U.S., at the end of *Preface to a Twenty Volume Suicide
Note*, the exile is once again complete: "Notes for a Speech" beginning "African
blues / does not know me. Their steps, in sands / of their own / land. A country
/ in black & white, newspapers / blown down pavements . . .," and concluding
with the reductive and terrible "democratic vista" of lower-case nationality:

> They shy away. My own
> dead souls, my, so called
> people. Africa

is a foreign place. You are
as any other sad man here
american.

Baraka's first book underscores how the scrutiny of poetic language com-
pelled him to redefine the ideological stance of the poet. Some ten years later,
after his Nationalist phase, this research will ultimately bring him to a kind of
Internationalism, a Third World Socialist aesthetic of liberation. First and fore-
most, up through his most recent poems, there will remain a critical, often rest-
less lyricism that insists, to borrow a phrase from Baraka's *Blues People*, that the
poem must "swing—from verb to noun."

Already in his second book, *The Dead Lecturer*, published in 1964 (the year
Dutchman is produced and wins an Obie, and not long before Baraka moves
from Greenwich Village to Harlem), there are several poems back-to-back at the
beginning of the collection in which the lyric is turned on itself, or rather on the
privileged figure of the poet ("Roi," as he signed himself until 1966).[6] In the
first, "Balboa, The Entertainer," the ironic title pushes a musical intensity, a
clarity of diction and phrasing, that is quite disarming:

> (The philosophers
> of need, of which
> I am lately
> one,
>   will tell you. "The People,"
> (and not think themselves
> liable
> to the same
> trembling flesh). I say now, "The People,
> as some lesson repeated, now,
> the lights are off, to myself,
> as a lover, or at the cold wind.

---

[6] Baraka was born Everett LeRoy Jones; the middle name LeRoi to appear in the fifties.

The next poem, "A Contract. (For the Destruction and Rebuilding of Paterson," revisits the populist language of Williams's civic icon (also Baraka's not so idyllic home state) in order to demolish it from within. The poet finds it crucial to attack "Paterson's" imaginative and mythopoetic core, in rebuilding a secular, more democratic and demytholigized city—and by extension, poetry—for those who must necessarily live within its limits:

> Flesh, and cars, tar, dug holes beneath stone
> a rude hierarchy of money, band saws cross out
> music, feeling. Even speech, corrodes.
> 　　　　　　　　　　　　　I came here
> from where I sat boiling in my veins, cold fear
> at the death of men, the death of learning, in
> cold fear, at my own. Romantic vests of same death
> blank at the corner, blank when they raise their fingers
>
> Cross the hearts, in dark flesh staggered so marvelous
> are their lies.

The rest of *The Dead Lecturer* is full of a lyrical multiplicity of rhythms and dictions that by decade's end will make Baraka a preeminent voice in American poetry. Accent and poetic stance, subject matter and ideological reflection are ever in the foreground as the poet is intent on clearing the air of Cold War social and cultural institutions. Along with many of his contemporaries outside the United States, Baraka continued to work from the assumptions of a highly politicized avant-garde. The ideological lucidity which generally defined the Third World and European poetries of the 1960s claimed the right of the poetic act to establish itself as the "conscience of communication."[7] The poem was conceived as a total, linguistic act, uniquely capable of posing the problem of language: a human product critical of, and invaded by, mass media, government, etc., as well as remaining a primary symptom of reality. "The Politics of Rich Painters," for example, displays an articulate line or statement, driven by the

[7] Adriano Spatola, "A Vaguely Ontological Aspiration," *Invisible City,* 16/17 (June 1975), p. 33; translated and reprinted from *TamTam,* 2 (Parma, 1972).

nuances of shifting and heterogeneous cadences, often spoken, often collaged, always relentlessly material and public, that will characterize Baraka's writing throughout the rest of the decade:

> Just their fingers' prints
> staining the cold glass, is sufficient
> for commerce, and a proper ruling on
> humanity. You know the pity
> of democracy, that we must sit here
> and listen to how he made his money.
> Tho the catlogue of his possible ignorance
> roars and extends through the room
> like fire. "Love," becomes the pass,
> the word taken intimately to combat
> all the uses of language. So that learning
> itself falls into disrepute.

Thus, the leap in 1969 from *The Dead Lecturer* to *Black Magic*, the quintessential volume of his Nationalist period and one of the most influential publications of the 1960s' Black Arts movement, does not seem now as extreme as many in the literary establishment would have it. The ideological concern and intensity of earlier verse, such as "A Guerrilla Handbook," can hardly be dismissed as bohemian:

> Silent political rain
> against the speech
> of friends. (we love them
> trapped in life, knowing no way out
> except description. Or black soil
> floating in the arm.
> > We must convince the living
> > that the dead
> > cannot sing.

The hard-driving cadences of "Green Lantern's Solo" are not so different from the impetus of self-critical pieces in the first two sections of *Black Magic*, "Sabotage" and "Target Study":

No, Nigger, no, blind drunk in SantaSurreal's beard. Dead
hero
for our time who would advance the nation's economy by poking
holes
in his arms. As golden arms build a forest of loves, and find only
the heavy belly breath of ladies whispering their false
pregnancies through the
phone.

The political knowledge and the recasting of the rhetorical figure of the poet, which Baraka had set in motion in the earlier collection, bear fruit in the clarity of later compositions such as "Letter to E. Franklin Frazier":

Those days I rose through the smoke of chilling Saturdays
hiding my eyes from the shine boys, my mouth and my flesh
from their sisters. I walked quickly and always alone
watching the cheap city like I thought it would swell
and explode, and only my crooked breath could put it together
again.

The same applies to the dire, almost prosaic, reflective energy that concludes "The People Burning." The scrutiny of the poet not only embraces the poem, but questions the very self-consciousness itself of the poetic act, the difficulty of building poetry on what Walter Benjamin calls "individual renunciation":[8]

Sit down and forget it. Lean on your silence, breathing
the dark. Forget your whole life, pop your fingers in a closed room,
hopped-up witch doctor for the cowards of a recent generation. It is
choice, now, like a philsophy problem. It is choice, now, and
the weight is specific and personal. It is not an emotional decision.
There are facts, and who was it said, that this a scientific century.

[8] Walter Benjamin, "Addendum to 'The Paris in the Second Empire of Baudelaire,'" *Invisible City*, 21/22 (November 1977), p. 33.

Thus, what Baraka said of his former nationalist politics as he helped, in 1973-74, transform the Congress of Afrikan Peoples into a Marxist-Leninist organization, is what might be said of his poetics from then to the present. After publically altering what he termed his "narrow nationalist and bourgeois nationalist stand," repudiating it as, in fact, "reactionary,"[9] Baraka has gone on to point out that his intentions as a Third World Socialist are fundamentally like those he held as a Nationalist:

> They were similar in the sense I see art as a weapon of revolution. It's just now that I define revolution in Marxist terms. I once defined revolution in Nationalist terms. But I came to my Marxist view as a result of having struggled as a Nationalist and found certain dead ends theoretically and ideologically, as far as Nationalism was concerned and had to reach out for a communist ideology.[10]

So with the Marxist poetry from his later collections: *Hard Facts* (1975), *Poetry for the Advanced* (1979), *reggae or not!* (1981), the limited edition *In the Tradition* (1982) and the long poem *Why's/Wise* (1995). Specifically, with the last two titles, poetic and political projects conjoin in a genesis and almost operatic celebration of African-American music.

After the break with cultural Nationalism, Baraka has emerged as an artist in the international, progressive tradition of Cesar Vallejo, Luis Aragon, Paul Eluard, Aimé Césaire, and René Depestre. With the insistence that poetry be an active, socio-linguistic force, Baraka has pursued, since the early 1970s, a utopian Communist direction, much like what Aragon and Eluard called "lyrical communism." Within this dynamic, Baraka's writing continually seeks allegiance between what is radical or subversive politically and what is avant-garde poetically.

Moreover, as an African-American poet, his career embodies a commitment, along with poets like Césaire and Depestre, to develop a space within this internationalism for the spirit of negritude. For Baraka, negritude plays at the heart

---

[9] KPFK, Los Angeles radio interview, March 1976; transcribed in part in *Invisible City*, 23/25 (March 1979), p. 8
[10] *The Amiri Baraka/LeRoi Jones Reader*, p. xxviii.

of late twentieth-century poetics, animating and transforming what remains avant-garde in the project of Socialist literature. As Depestre writes, "The new Black Orpheus will be a revolutionary or he will be nothing at all."[11]

Many have underscored the exemplar of contemporary jazz in Baraka's work, how it has provided a model of a genuinely avant-idiom, taking from European and Third World art practices alike, to form its own singular, African-American mode. In this regard, Baraka characterizes what for him, at the close of a century, is fresh and contemporary:

> If you're a modern artist who's not some kind of cultural nationalist, you understand that you can learn from anything and anybody, see that the whole of world culture is at your disposal, because no one people has created the monuments of art and culture in the world, it's been collective.[12]

More recent work, such as the selection here from *Why's/Wise*, show music and history to be almost indivisible as subjects of poetry. Baraka's chronicles of African-American culture establish a new standard, a mode of composition that is, in its temporal and geographical vision, truly "multinational."[13] The lyricism of the early books has been challenged and extended to where it is inseparable from his thought, ideological or otherwise. It has become, as he wrote in eulogy of Miles Davis, "a prayer in the future."[14] Baraka's is a verbal music that presages and defines what is to come.

[11] Speech to the Tricontinental Cultural Congress in Havana, 1967, reprinted in *Invisible City*, 10 (October 1973), p. 9

[12] KGNU, Boulder, Colorado, broadcast, July 27, 1984; transcribed in part in the *Amiri Baraka/LeRoi Jones Reader*, pp. 249-50

[13] Ibid, p. 250.

[14] "When Miles Split!," forthcoming in *Eulogies*, New York: Marsilio, 1996; originally in *Sulfur*, 30 (Spring 1992), p. 5.

TRANSBLUESENCY

PREFACE TO A TWENTY VOLUME
SUICIDE NOTE. . . .

Preface to a Twenty Volume Suicide Note

(For Kellie Jones, born 16 May 1959)

Lately, I've become accustomed to the way
The ground opens up and envelopes me
Each time I go out to walk the dog.
On the broad edged silly music the wind
Makes when I run for a bus . . .

Things have come to that.

And now, each night I count the stars,
And each night I get the same number.
And when they will not come to be counted,
I count the holes they leave.

Nobody sings anymore.

And then last night, I tiptoed up
To my daughter's room and heard her
Talking to someone, and when I opened
The door, there was no one there . . .
Only she on her knees, peeking into

Her own clasped hands.

March 1957

Hymn for Lanie Poo

Vous êtes des faux Nègres
                        —Rimbaud

O,
these wild trees
will make charming wicker baskets,
the young woman
the young black woman
the young black beautiful woman
said.

> These wild-assed trees
> will make charming
> wicker baskets.

(now, I'm putting words in her mouth . . . tch)

I

All afternoon
we watched the cranes
humping each other
                    dropped
                    our shadows
                    onto the beach
and covered them over with sand.

Beware the evil sun . . .
turn you black

turn your hair

crawl your eyeballs

rot your teeth.

All afternoon
we sit around
near the edge of the city
                    hacking open
                    crocodile skulls
                    sharpening our teeth.

The god I pray to
got black boobies
got steatopygia

make faces in the moon
make me a greenpurple &
maroon winding sheet.
                    I wobble out to
                    the edge of the water

give my horny yell
& 24 elephants
stomp out of the subway
with consecrated hardons.

(watch out for that evil sun
turn you black)
               My fireface

my orange

and fireface
squat by the flames.
She had her coming out party
with 3000 guests
from all parts of the country.
Queens, Richmond, Togoland, The Camerooons;
A white hunter, very unkempt,
with long hair,
whizzed in on the end of a vine.
(spoke perfect english too.)

"Throw on another goddamned Phoenecian,"
I yelled, really getting with it.

John Coltrane arrived with an Egyptian lady.
he played very well.

"Throw on another goddamned Phoenecian."

We got so drunk (Hulan Jack
brought his bottle of Thunderbird),
nobody went hunting
the next morning.

   2

o,
don't be shy honey.
we all know
these wicker baskets
would make wild-assed trees.

Monday, I spent most of the day hunting
Knocked off about six, gulped down a cou-
ple of monkey foreskins, then took in a
flick. Got to bed early.

Tuesday, same thing all day. (Caught a
mangy lioness with one tit.) Ate.
Watched television for awhile. Read the
paper, then hit the sack.

Wednesday, took the day off.
Took the wife and kids to the games.
Read Garmanda's book, "14 Tribes of
Ambiguity," didn't like it.

Thursday, we caught a goddamn ape.
Must've weighed about 600 pounds.
We'll probably eat ape meat for the
rest of the month. Christ, I hate
ape meat.

Friday, I stayed home with a supposed
cold. Goofed the whole day trying to
rethatch the roof. Had run in with
the landlord.

We spent the weekend at home.
I tried to get some sculpting done,
but nothing came of it. It's impos-
sible to be an artist and a bread
winner at the same time.
Sometimes I think I oughta chuck
the whole business.

3

The firemasons parade.

(The sun is using this country
as a commode.

Beware the sun, my love.)

The firemasons are very square.
They are supposed to be a civic
and fraternal organization, but
all they do is have parades and
stay high. They also wear funny
looking black hats, which are
round and have brims. The fire-
masons are cornballs.

4

Each morning
I go down
to Gansevoort St.
and stand on the docks.
I stare out
at the horizon
until it gets up
and comes to embrace
me. I
make believe
it is my father.

This is known
as genealogy.

5

We came into the
silly little church
shaking our wet raincoats
on the floor.
It wasn't water,
that made the raincoats
wet.
    The preacher's
    conning eyes
    filed when he saw
    the way I walked to-
    wards him; almost
    throwing my hips out
    of whack.
    He screamed,

He's wet with the blood of the lamb!!

And everybody
got real happy.

6 (die schwartze Bohemien)

They laught,

and religion was something

he fount in coffee ships, by God.

It's not that I got enything
against cotton, nosiree, by God

It's just that . . .
                    Man lookatthatblonde
                                        whewee!

I think they are not treating us like

Mr. Lincun said they should
                            or Mr. Gandhi

For that matter. By God.

                    ZEN

is a bitch! Like "Bird" was,
                            Cafe Olay

for me, Miss.

                    But white cats can't swing . . .

Or the way this guy kept patronizing me—

like he was Bach or somebody

                            Oh, I knew

John Kasper when he hung around with shades . . .

She's a painter, Man.

It's just that it's such a drag to go
Way uptown for Bar B Cue,

By God . . .

How much?

7

About my sister.

(O, generation revered
above all others.
O, generation of fictitious
Ofays

I revere you . . .
You are all so beautiful)

my sister drives a green jaguar
my sister has her hair done twice a month
my sister is a school teacher
my sister took ballet lessons
my sister has a fine figure: never diets
my sister doesn't like to teach in Newark
    because there are too many colored
    in her classes
my sister hates loud shades
my sister's boy friend is a faggot music teacher
    who digs Tschaikovsky
my sister digs Tschaikovsky also
it is because of this similarity of interests
that they will probably get married.

Smiling & glad/in
the huge & loveless
white-anglo sun/of
benevolent step
mother America.

In Memory of Radio

Who has ever stopped to think of the divinity of Lamont Cranston?
(Only Jack Kerouac, that I know of: & me.
The rest of you probably had on WCBS and Kate Smith,
Or something equally unattractive.)

What can I say?
It is better to have loved and lost
Than to put linoleum in your living rooms?

Am I a sage or something?
Mandrake's hypnotic gesture of the week?
(Remember, I do not have the healing powers of Oral Roberts . . .
I cannot, like F. J. Sheen, tell you how to get saved *& rich!*
I cannot even order you to gaschamber satori like Hitler or
        Goody Knight

& Love is an evil word.
Turn it backwards/see, see what I mean?
An evol word. & besides
who understands it?
I certainly wouldn't like to go out on that kind of limb.

Saturday mornings we listened to *Red Lantern* & his undersea folk.
At II, *Let's Pretend*/& we did/& I, the poet, still do, Thank God!

What was it he used to say (after the transformation, when he was safe
& invisible & the unbelievers couldn't throw stones?) "Heh, heh, heh,
Who knows what evil lurks in the hearts of men? The Shadow knows."

O, yes he does
O, yes he does.
An evil word it is,
This Love.

Look for You Yesterday,
Here You Come Today

Part of my charm:

                  envious blues feeling
                  separation of church & state
                  grim calls from drunk debutantes

Morning never aids me in my quest.
I have to trim my beard in solitude.
I try to hum lines from "The Poet In New York".

People saw metal all around the house on Saturdays. The Phone
                                          rings.

terrible poems come in the mail. Descriptions of celibate parties
                      torn trousers: Great Poets dying
                      with their strophes on. & me
                      incapable of a simple straightforward
                      anger.

It's so diffuse
being alive. Suddenly one is aware
              that nobody really gives a damn.
              My wife is pregnant with *her* child.
              "It means nothing to me", sez Strindberg.

An avalanche of words
could cheer me up. Words from Great Sages.
                    Was James Karolis a great sage??

Why did I let Ora Matthews beat him up
in the bathroom? Haven't I learned my lesson.

I would take up painting
if I cd think of a way to do it
better than Leonardo. Than Bosch
Than Hogarth. Than Kline.

Frank walked off the stage, singing
"My silence is as important as Jack's incessant yatter."

I am a mean hungry sorehead.
Do I have the capacity for grace??

To arise one smoking spring
& find one's youth has taken off
for greener parts.

A sudden blankness in the day
as if there were no afternoon.
& all my piddling joys retreated
to their own dopey mythic worlds.

The hours of the atmosphere
grind their teeth like hags.

(When will world war two be over?)

I stood up on a mailbox
waving my yellow tee-shirt
watching the grey tanks
stream up Central Ave.

All these thots
are Flowers Of Evil
cold & lifeless
as subway rails

the sun like a huge cobblestone
flaking its brown slow rays
primititi
        once, twice, . My life
        seems over & done with.
        Each morning I rise
        like a sleep walker
        & rot a little more.

All the lovely things I've known have disappeared.
I have all my pubic hair & am lonely.
There is probably no such place as BattleCreek, Michigan!

Tom Mix dead in a Boston Nightclub
before I realized what happened.

People laugh when I tell them about Dickie Dare!
What is one to do in an alien planet
where the people breath New Ports?
Where is my space helmet, I sent for it
3 lives ago . . . when there were box tops.

What has happened to box tops??

O, God . . . I must have a belt that glows green
in the dark. Where is my Captain Midnight decoder??
I can't understand what Superman is saying!

THERE *MUST* BE A LONE RANGER!!!

****

but this also
is part of my charm.
A maudlin nostalgia
that comes on
like terrible thoughts about death.

How dumb to be sentimental about anything
To call it love
& cry pathetically
into the long black handkerchief
of the years.

        "Look for you yesterday
        Here you come today
        Your mouth wide open
        But what you got to say?"

           —part of my charm

               old envious   blues feeling
               ticking like   a big cobblestone clock.

I hear the reel running out . . .
the spectators are impatient for popcorn:
It was only a selected short subject

F. Scott Charon
will soon be glad-handing me
like a legionaire

My silver bullets all gone
My black mask trampled in the dust

& Tonto way off in the hills
moaning like Bessie Smith.

To a Publisher . . . Cut-out

The blight rests in your face.
For your unknown musiks. The care & trust
Undeliberate. Like an axe-murder
Or flat pancake. The night cold & asexual
A long sterile moon lapping at the dank Hudson.
The end of a star. The water more than any
Other thing. We are dibbled here. Seurat's
Madness. That kind of joke. Isolate
Land creatures in a wet unfriendly world.

We must be strong. (smoke Balkan Sobranie)
People will think you have the taste
In this hyar family. Some will stroke your face.
Better posture is another thing. Watch out for Peanuts,
he's gonna turn out bad/ A J.D./ A Beatnik/ A
Typical wise-ass N.Y. kid. "X" wanted to bet me
that Charlie Brown spent most of his time
whacking his doodle, or having weird relations
with that dopey hound of his (though that's
a definite improvement over "Arf Arf" & that
filthy little lesbian hes hung up with.)

As if any care could see us through. Could defend us.
Save us from you, Little Darling. Or me, which is worse.
"A far far worser thing I do/than I has ever done".
Put that in your pipe & watch out for the gendarmes.
They arresses people for less than that. For less
Than we are ever capable of. Any kind of sincerity

Guarantees complete disregard. Complete abnegation.
"Must dig with my fingers/as nobody will lend me
or sell me a pick axe." Axe the man who owns one.
Hellzapoppin. The stars might not come on tonight . . .
& who the hell can do anything about that?? Eh,
Milord/ Milady/ The kind Dubarry wasn't. Tres slick.

But who am I to love anybody? I ride the 14th St. bus
every day . . . reading Hui neng/ Raymond Chandler/ Olson . . .
I have slept with almost every mediocre colored woman
On 23rd St . . . At any rate, talked a good match. And
Frightened by the lack of any real communication
I addressed several perfumed notes to Uncle Don
& stuffed them into the radio. In the notes,
Of course, crude assignations, off color suggestions,
Diagrams of new methods for pederasts, lewd poems
That rime. IF ONLY HE WOULD READ THESE ON THE AIR.
(There are other things could take my mind from
this childe's play . . . but none nearly as interesting.)

I long to be a mountain climber
& wave my hands up 8,000 feet.
Out of sight & snow blind/the tattered
Stars and Stripes poked in the new peak.

& come down later, Clipper by my side,
To new wealth & eternal fame. That
Kind of care. I could wear
Green corduroy coats & felt tyroleans
For the rest of my days; & belong to clubs.

Grandeur in boldness. Big & stupid as the wind.
But so lovely. Who's to understand that kind of con?

As if each day, after breakfast, someone asked you,
"What do you want to be when you grow up??" &
Day in, Day out, you just kept belching.

Ostriches & Grandmothers!

All meet here with us, finally: the
uptown, way-west, den of inconstant
moralities.
Faces up: all
my faces turned up
to the sun.

I

Summer's mist nods against the trees
till distance grows in my head
like an antique armada
dangled motionless from the horizon.

Unbelievable changes. Restorations.
Each day like my niña's fan
tweaking the flat air
back and forth till the room
is a blur of flowers.

Intimacy takes on human form . . .
& sheds it like a hide.
                              Lips, eyes,
tiny lace coughs
reflected on night's stealth.

2

Tonight, one star.
eye of the dragon.
          The Void
signaling.
Reminding someone
it's still there.

3

It's these empty seconds
I fill with myself. Each
a recognition. A complete
utterance.

Here, it is color; motion;
the feeling of dazzling beauty
Flight.

As
the trapeeze rider
leans
with arms spread

wondering at the bar's
delay

Scenario VI

. . . and I come out of it
with this marvelous yellow cane
in my hand, yellow cashmere jacket
green felt pants & green boater . . . & green &
black clack shoes, polished & fast, jiggling
in the wings . . . till Vincente says "rollllem"
& I jiggle out on the stage, hands in my pockets,
the cane balanced delicately under my arm, spinning
& clack clack clacking across the bare sunday clothesline
tilting the hat to avoid the sun & ginergerly missing
the dried branch I had put there yesterday.

The motion of the mind! Smooooth; I jiggle
& clack stomping one foot & the clothesline swings.
Fabulei Verwachsenes. Ripping this one off
in a series of dramatic half-turns I learned
many years ago in the orient; Baluba:
"The power to cloud men's minds" &c., which
I'm sure you must have heard about, doodle-doo.
& then I'm sitting in this red chair, humming,
feet still pecking at the marble floor, the
line motionless with only the tiniest leaf
on the dead branch waving, slowly; With a red background,
& I can't see anything, only hear this raspy 1936 voice
singing in german a very groovy love song; to me.

There's a train whistle, too. In and out like this.
When out the open window of early spring, sharp

browns & greens fuzzy through the shade
& a fence somehow too bleak to describe, or even
be made sad by.

& I'm not even breathing hard. Tapping my feet
so nicely, the cane too, on the red marble. No
echo, that's distant thunder for these early summer storms,
cools off the whole scene too. But waiting
for my next cue, Vincente comes over, lights my cigarette,
We make a date for next wednesday, at the rainbow hut,
& he has a fabulous cigarette holder. & he pats
my cane-hand & says, "you do it up, baby". I'm on again.

Sylvia has come out in her smashing oranges & jewelry,
she has her mouth wide & I can hear her listening to
my feet clackings for her deep beauty doesn't include
rhythm. But we make it in great swirls out to the terrace,
which overlooks Sumer . . . & the Indus river, where next
week probably all kinds of white trash will ride in
on stolen animals we will be amazed by.

Way Out West

(For Gary Snyder)

As simple an act
as opening the eyes. Merely
coming into things by degrees.

Morning: some tear is broken
on the wooden stairs
of my lady's eyes. Profusions
of green. The leaves. Their
constant prehensions. Like old
junkies on Sheridan Square, eyes
cold and round. There is a song
Nat Cole sings . . . This city
& the intricate disorder
of the seasons.

Unable to mention
something as abstract as time.

Even so, (bowing low in thick
smoke from cheap incense; all
kinds questions filling the mouth,
till you suffocate & fall dead
to opulent carpet.) Even so,

shadows will creep over your flesh
& hide your disorder, your lies.

There are unattractive wild ferns
outside the window
where the cats hide. They yowl
from there at nights. In heat
& bleeding on my tulips.

Steel bells, like the evil
unwashed Sphinx, towing in the twilight.
Childless old murderers, for centuries
with musty eyes.

I am distressed. Thinking
of the seasons, how they pass,
how I pass, my very youth, the
ripe sweet of my life; drained off . . .

Like giant rhesus monkeys;
picking their skulls,
with ingenious cruelty
sucking out the brains.

No use for beauty
collapsed, with moldy breath
done in. Insidious weight
of cankered dreams. Tiresias'
weathered cock.

Walking into the sea, shells
caught in the hair. Coarse
waves tearing the tongue.

Closing the eyes. As
simple an act. You float

The Bridge

(# for wieners & mcclure)

I have forgotten the head
of where I am. Here at the bridge. 2
bars, down the street, seeming
to wrap themselves around my fingers, the day,
screams in me; pitiful like a little girl
you sense will be dead before the winter
is over.

I can't see the bridge now, I've past
it, its shadow, we drove through, headed out
along the cold insensitive roads to what
we wanted to call "ourselves."
"How does the bridge go?" Even tho
you find yourself in its length
strung out along its breadth, waiting
for the cold sun to tear out your eyes. Enamoured
of its blues, spread out in the silk clubs of
this autumn tune. The changes are difficult, when
you hear them, & know they are all in you, the chords

of your disorder meddle with your would be disguises.
Sifting in, down, upon your head, with the sun & the insects.

(Late feeling) Way down till it barely, after that rush of
wind & odor reflected from hills you have forgotten the color
when you touch the water, & it closes, slowly, around your head.

The bridge will be behind you, that music you know, that place,
you feel when you look up to say, it is me, & I have forgotten,
all the things, you told me to love, to try to understand, the
bridge will stand, high up in the clouds & the light, & you,

(when you have let the song run out) will be sliding through
unmentionable black.

Vice

Sometimes I feel I have to express myself
and then, whatever it is I have to express
falls out of my mouth like flakes of ash
from a match book that the drunken guest
at the grey haired jew lady's birthday party has
set on fire, for fun & to ease the horrible boredom.

& when these flakes amass, I make serious collages
or empty them (feinting a gratuitous act) out the window
on the heads of the uncurious puerto rican passersby.

ACT I. The celibate bandit pees in the punch bowl.

(curious image) occurring friday evening, a house
full of middle class women & a photogenic baker.
Baby bear has eaten her porridge, had her bath, shit
& gone to sleep. Smoke rises (strange for mid-summer)
out of a strange little shack in the middle of the
torn down cathedral. Everything seems to be light green.
I suppose, a color of despair or wretchedness. Anyway,
everything is light green, even the curling little hairs
on the back of my hand, and the old dog scar glinting
in the crooked (green, light green) rays of an unshaded bulb.

There doesn't seem to be any act 2. The process is stopped.
Functional, as a whip, a strong limb broken off in the gale
lying twisty & rotten, unnoticed in my stone back yard.
All this means nothing is happening to me (in this world).

I suppose some people are having a ball. Organized fun.
Pot Smokers Institute is going on an outing tomorrow; my
corny sister, in her fake bohemian pants, is borrowing something
else. (A prestige item). These incomprehensible dullards!

Asked to be special, & alive in the mornings, if they are green
& I am still alive, (& green) hovering above all the things I
seem to want to be apart of (curious smells, the high-noon idea
of life . . . a crowded train station where they broadcast a slice,
just one green slice, of some glamourous person's life).
& I cant even isolate my pleasures. All the things I can talk about
mean nothing to me.

This is *not* rage. (I am not that beautiful!) Only immobile coughs
& gestures towards somethings I don't understand. If I were lucky
enough to still be an adolescent, I'd just attribute these weird
singings in my intestine to sex, & slink off merrily to mastur
bate. Mosaic of disorder I own but cannot recognize. Mist in me.

There must be some great crash in the slinky world: MYSTIC CURE . . .
Cunning panacea of the mind. The faith of it. the singed hairs
of human trust, corrupt & physical as a disease. A glass stare.

Resolution, for the quick thrust of epee, to force your opponent
cringing against the wall, not in anger, but unfettered happiness
while your lady is watching from the vined balcony, your triumph.

& years after, you stand in subways watching your invincible hand
bring the metal to bear again & again, when you are old & the lady,
(o, fond memories we hide in our money belts, & will not spend)
the lady, you young bandits who have not yet stolen your first purse

the lady will be dead.

And if you are alone (if there is something in you so cruel)

You will wonder at the extravagance

of youth.

Symphony Sid

First
take the first
thing. Blue. The mountain,
largest of our
landscape. From
a dark hall at
the bottom, the shapes
a shadow, without
hardness, or that
ugly smell of
blackening flesh.
                    The scale
is music, black shadow
from highest wild
fingers placing evening
beneath our
tongues.
            A man, a woman
shaking the night apart. Forget
who you are. Forget
my fingers.

Betancourt

(For Rubi)

What are
influences?
               A green truck
wet & glowing, seance
of ourselves, elegy for the sea
at night, my flesh
a woman's, at the fingertips
soft white increased coolness
from the dark
sea.
        We sat
with our backs
to the sea. Not
in the gardens
of Spain, but some
new greenness, birds
scorching the yellow
rocks at the foot
of the sea's wall. A barrier
of rock, tilting backwards, damp,
thrown up against
a floating dreary
disgust. Even fear
without that self possession. The
night's defection. Walking all night
entwined inside, I mean
I tasted you, your real & fleshy

voice
inside my head
& choked
as if some primitive
corruption re-sat
itself in full view
of a puritan flame. And flame
is the mind, the wet hands
mark on strange islands
of warmth.
       Big stone nose, nigger
lips, the entire head
thrust from
a serpents snout. Idle
somehow, fire scorching
the plain earth we pulled
up around thinking
to limit its violence. To
contain even that
madness (within
some thrown wall
of words.)
       Our gestures
are silence. The sea's
wet feathers slowly
black. (You die
from mornings, looking down
from that silence
at the silence
of roofs. Disconnected
flesh. Not even cars
from this distance
are real.

2

This
is slower. Infused (somehow)
with sound
& distance. Slow

the cock
flat
on skin
like
a dead
insect. A
bee, with
crushed
antlers,
sprawled
on its side,
              And last night, talking to ourselves, except
when some wildness
cut us, ripped impossibly
deep beneath black
flesh
to black bone. Then
we loved each other. Understood
the miles of dead air
between our
softest parts. French girl
from the desert. Desert man,
whose mind is some rotting
country of snow.

3

There is more
underneath. Rotted, green
beneath hands making
their deadly wishes
show. La casa. El edificio. La
Mar. El hombre. Without seething
tin braziers, no, those weird cups
in novels: chalices.

                  I was reading
some old man's poems
this morning. A lover
hid himself under
the stink of low trailing
sea birds, heavy sun, pure
distance. He had to go away,
I mean, from all of us, even
you, marvelous person
at the sea's edge. Even you
Sra. de Jiminez. Rubi.

              And

I think he knew
all this would happen, that
when I dropped the book
the sky would have already
moved, turned black, and
wet grey air
would mark the windows.

                    That

there are fools
who hang close

to their original
thought. Elementals
of motion (Not, again,
that garden) but some
slightness
of feeling
they think is sweet
and long to die
inside.
   Think
about it! As even
this, now, a turning
away. (I mean I think
I know now
what a poem
is) A
turning away . . .
from what
it was
had moved
us . . .
   A
madness.
    Looking at the sea. And some
white fast boat.

30 July 1960
Habana

The Insidious Dr. Fu Man Chu

If I think myself
strong, then I am
not true to the misery
in my life. The uncertainty.
(of what I am saying, who
I have chose to become, the
very air pressing my skin
held gently away, this woman
and the one I taste continually
in my nebular pallet tongue face
mouth feet, standing in piles
of numbers, hills, lovers.
                                    If
I think myself ugly
& go to the mirror, smiling,
at the inaccuracy, or now
the rain pounds dead grass
in the stone yard, I think
how very wise I am. How very
very wise.

The New Sheriff

There is something
in me so cruel, so
silent. It hesitates
to sit on the grass
with the young white
                    virgins
of my time. The blood-
letter, clothed in what
it is. Elemental essence,
animal grace, not that, but
a rude stink of color
huger, more vast, than
this city suffocating. Red
street. Waters noise
in the ear, inside
the hard bone
of the brain. Inside
the soft white meat
of the feelings. Inside
your flat white stomach
I move my tongue

From an Almanac

In the nature
of flesh, these clown gods
are words, blown
in the winters, thou
windows, lacking
sun.
      In the nature,
of ideas, in the nature of
words, these
clown god's are
winter. Are blown
thru our windows.
                The flesh
& bone
of the season. Each
dead thing
hustled
across the pavement. Each
dead word
drowned
in a winter wind. Are
in the nature
of flesh. These
liars, clown
gods

From an Almanac (2)

Respect the season
and dance to the rattle
of its bones.
                    The flesh
hung
from trees. Blown
down. A cold
music. A colder
hand, will grip
you. Your bare
soul. (Where is the soul's place. What is
its
nature?) Winter rattles
like the throat
of the hanged man. Swung
against our windows.
                    As bleak
as our thots. As wild
as that wind
we make (between
us).
        Can you dance? Shall
you?

From an Almanac (3)

(For C.O.)

This bizness, of dancing, how
can it suit us? Old men, naked
sterile women.
                    (our time,
a cruel one. Our soul's warmth
left out. Little match children,
dance
against the weather.
) The soul's
warmth
is how
shall I say
it,
        Its own. A place
of warmth, for children
wd dance there,
                    if they cd. If they
left their brittle selves behind (our time's
a cruel one.
            Children
of winter. (I cross myself
like religion
            Children
of a cruel time. (the wind
stirs the bones
& they drag clumsily
thru the cold.)

These children
are older
than their worlds. and
cannot dance.

Notes for a Speech

African blues
does not know me. Their steps, in sands
of their own
land. A country
in black & white, newspapers
blown down pavements
of the world. Does
not feel
what I am.
        Strength
in the dream, an oblique
suckling of nerve, the wind
throws up sand, eyes
are something locked in
hate, of hate, of hate, to
walk abroad, they conduct
their deaths apart
from my own. Those
heads, I call
my "people."
        (And who are they. People. To concern
myself, ugly man. Who
you, to concern
the white flat stomachs
of maidens, inside houses
dying. Black. Peeled moon
light on my fingers
move under

her clothes. Where
is her husband. Black
words throw up sand
to eyes, fingers of
their private dead. Whose
soul, eyes, in sand. My color
is not theirs. Lighter, white man
talk. They shy away. My own
dead souls, my, so called
people. Africa
is a foreign place. You are
as any other sad man here
american.

THE DEAD LECTURER

As a Possible Lover

Practices
silence, the way of wind
bursting
its early lull. Cold morning
to night, we go so
slowly, without
thought
to ourselves. (Enough
to have thought
tonight, nothing
finishes it. What
you are, will have
no certainty, or
end. That you will
stay, where you are,
a human gentle wisp
of life. Ah . . .)
                  practices
loneliness,
as a virtue. A single
specious need
to keep
what you have
never really
had.

Balboa, the Entertainer

It cannot come
except you make it
from materials
it is not
caught from. (The philosophers
of need, of which
I am lately
one,
     will tell you. "The People,"
(and not think themselves
liable
to the same
trembling flesh). I say now, "The People,
as some lesson repeated, now,
the lights are off, to myself,
as a lover, or at the cold wind.

Let my poems be a graph
of me. (And they keep
to the line, where flesh
drops off. You will go
blank at the middle. A
dead man.

       But
die soon, Love. If
what you have for
yourself, does not

stretch to your body's
end.
    (Where, without
preface,
music trails, or your fingers
slip
from my arm

A Contract. (For the Destruction and Rebuilding of Paterson

Flesh, and cars, tar, dug holes beneath stone
a rude hierarchy of money, band saws cross out
music, feeling. Even speech, corrodes.
                              I came here
from where I sat boiling in my veins, cold fear
at the death of men, the death of learning, in
cold fear, at my own. Romantic vests of same death
blank at the corner, blank when they raise their fingers

Criss the hearts, in dark flesh staggered so marvelous
are their lies. So complete, their mastery, of these
stupid niggers. Loud spics kill each other, and will not

make the simple trip to Tiffany's. Will not smash their stainless
heads, against the simpler effrontery of so callous a code as gain.

You are no brothers, dirty woogies, dying under dried rinds, in massa's
droopy tuxedos. Cab Calloways of the soul, at the soul's juncture, a
music, they think will save them from our eyes. (In back of the terminal

where the circus will not go. At the backs of crowds, stooped and vulgar
breathing hate syllables, unintelligible rapes of all that linger in
our new world. Killed in white fedora hats, they stand so mute at what

whiter slaves did to my father. They muster silence. They pray at the
steps of abstract prisons, to be kings, when all is silence, when all
is stone. When even the stupid fruit of their loins is gold, or something
else they cannot eat.

This Is the Clearing I Once Spoke of

The talk scared him. Left alone, with me,
at some water. (Suddenness of your mind,
because you will be saved. Stand there
counting deaths. My own, is what I wanted
you to say, Roi, you will die soon.)

                              And
it went well, till evening, and the birds
fled. Their trees hanging empty at the
river. All of it a creation. More than
ideas. The simple elegant hand, a man
will extend. More than we can lose, and
still talk lovingly of "ourselves."

The brush sank behind its silence. This
was a jungle, dead children of thought.
We sat looking, and the wind changed
our fire, it was blue, and sang slowly.

Whose mind has this here? The way love
will move. I love you, I say that now
evenly, without emotion. Having
lost you. Or sitting, at the ruptured
threads of light. Wind and birds, spurn
out over the water, silent or dead.

A Poem for Neutrals

A japanese neon landscape blinks
a constant film
of memory. His leaves, his hills
change in dumb perspective. Farmers
and Americans,
                    say they are blue. Some natural phenomenon
some possible image
of what we shall call history. A jungle
of feeling. In their minds, the broken
tree, wet blood in the romantic's bulb. our sudden
and misconceived beauty. Inept tenderness. (For
those long girls lay in darkness under our smell.
Those talkers who will **not** shut up
when the dawn comes. **And** stand in doorways
letting cold air blow in.
                    It is a history of motive,
as secure as the economy
for these restless dwarfs
performing miracles for the blind. The wet ring
on their pants
the menace
of our education. It is not Dante,
nor Yeats. But the loud and drunken
pilgrim, I knew so well
in my youth. And grew to stone
waiting for the change.

2

The calendar is memory. The dead roots
of the poet's brain. Yellow skin, black
skin, or the formless calm of compromise. They will not come
to see, or understand you. They will call you "murderer,"
as new songs for their young. The mountains
in your country, the flat skies of mine. (Except
by the oceans, the poor hate their shadows,
and force their agony to dance.

All night blue leaves ring
in Kyoto. And the windows of 5th street
scream.

An Agony. As Now

I am inside someone
who hates me. I look
out from his eyes. Smell
what fouled tunes come in
to his breath. Love his
wretched women.

Slits in the metal, for sun. Where
my eyes sit turning, at the cool air
the glance of light, or hard flesh
rubbed against me, a woman, a man,
without shadow, or voice, or meaning.

This is the enclosure (flesh,
where innocence is a weapon. An
abstraction. Touch. (Not mine.
Or yours, if you are the soul I had
and abandoned when I was blind and had
my enemies carry me as a dead man
(if he is beautiful, or pitied.

It can be pain. (As now, as all his
flesh hurts me.) It can be that. Or
pain. As when she ran from me into
that forest.
   Or pain, the mind
silver spiraled whirled against the
sun, higher than even old men thought

God would be. Or pain. And the other. The
yes. (Inside his books, his fingers. They
are withered yellow flowers and were never
beautiful.) The yes. You will, lost soul, say
'beauty.' Beauty, practiced, as the tree. The
slow river. A white sun in its wet sentences.
Or, the cold men in their gale. Ecstasy. Flesh
or soul. The yes. (Their robes blown. Their bowls
empty. They chant at my heels, not at yours.) Flesh
or soul, as corrupt. Where the answer moves too quickly.
Where the God is a self, after all.)

Cold air blown through narrow blind eyes. Flesh,
white hot metal. Glows as the day with its sun.
It is a human love, I live inside. A bony skeleton
you recognize as words or simple feeling.

But it has no feeling. As the metal, is hot, it is not,
given to love.

It burns the thing
inside it. And that thing
screams.

A Poem For Willie Best*

I

The face sings, alone
at the top
                    of the body. All
flesh, all song, aligned. For hell
is silent, at those cracked lips
flakes of skin and mind
twist and whistle softly
as they fall.
                    It was your own death
you saw. Your own face, stiff
and raw. This
without sound, or
movement. Sweet afton, the
dead beggar bleeds
yet. His blood, for a time
alive, and huddled in a door
way, struggling to sing. Rain
washes it into cracks. Pits
whose bottoms are famous. Whose sides
are innocent broadcasts
of another life.

* Willie Best was a Negro character actor whose Hollywood name was Sleep'n'eat.

II

At this point, neither
front nor back. A point, the
dimensionless line. The top
of a head, seen from Christ's
heaven, stripped of history
or desire.
        Fixed, perpendicular
to shadow. (even speech, vertical,
leaves no trace. Born in to death
held fast to it, where
the lover spreads his arms, the line
he makes to threaten Gods with history.
The fingers stretch to emptiness. At
each point, after flesh, even light
is speculation. But an end, his end,
failing a beginning.

2

A cross. The gesture, symbol, line
arms held stiff, nailed stiff, with
no sign, of what gave them strength.
The point, become a line, a cross, or
the man, and his material, driven in
the ground. If the head rolls back
and the mouth opens, screamed into
existence, there will be perhaps
only the slightest hint of movement—
a smear; no help will come. No one
will turn to that station again.

III

At a cross roads, sits the
player. No drum, no umbrella, even
though it's raining. Again, and we
are somehow less miserable because
here is a hero, used to being wet.
One road is where you are standing now
(reading this, the other, crosses then
rushes into a wood.

        5 lbs neckbones.
        5 lbs hog innards.
        10 bottles cheap wine.

                      (The contents

of a paper bag, also shoes, with holes
for the big toe, and several rusted
knives. This is a literature, of
symbols. And it is his gift, as the
bag is.
     (The contents
again, holy saviours,

        300 men on horseback
        75 bibles
        the quietness

of a field. A rich
man, though wet through
by the rain.
      I said,

        47 howitzers
        7 polished horses jaws
        a few trees being waved

softly back under
the black night

All This should be
invested.

IV

Where
ever,
he has gone. who ever
mourns
or sits silent
to remember

There is nothing of pity
here. Nothing
of sympathy.

V

This is the dance of the raised
leg. Of the hand on the knee
quickly.
As a dance it punishes
speech. 'The house burned. The
old man killed.'
As a dance it
is obscure.

VI

This is the song

of the highest C.
The falsetto. An elegance
that punishes silence. This is the song
of the toes pointed inward, the arms swung, the
hips, moved, for fucking, slow, from side
to side. He is quoted
saying, "My father was
never a jockey,
but

he did teach me
how to ride."

VII

The balance.
(Rushed in, swarmed of dark, cloaks,
and only red lights pushed a message
to the street. Rub.
This is the lady,
I saw you with.
This is your mother.
This is the lady I wanted
some how to sleep with.
As a dance, or
our elegant song. Sun red and grown
from trees, fences, mud roads in dried out
river beds. This is for me, with no God
but what is given. Give me.
Something more
than what is here. I must tell you
my body hurts.

The balance.

     Can you hear? Here
I am again. Your boy, dynamite. Can
you hear? My soul is moved. The soul
you gave me. I say, my soul, and it
is moved. That soul
you gave me.

     Yes, I'm sure
this is the lady. You
slept with her. Witness, your boy,
here, dynamite. Hear?

         I mean
can you?

The balance.

     He was tired of losing. (And
his walking buddies tired
of walking.

    Bent slightly,
at the waist. Left hand low, to flick
quick showy jabs ala Sugar. The right
cocked, to complete,

      any combination.

        He was
tired of losing, but he was fighting
a big dumb "farmer."

     Such a blue bright
afternoon, and only a few hundred yards
from the beach. He said, I'm tired
of losing.

   "I *got* ta cut 'cha."

VIII

A renegade
behind the mask. And even
the mask, a renegade
disguise. Black skin
and hanging lip.
                    Lazy
                    Frightened
                    Thieving
                    Very potent sexually
                    Scars
                    Generally inferior
                                        (but natural

rhythms.

His head is
at the window. The only
part
      that sings.

(The word he used
                    (we are passing St. Mark's place
                    and those crazy jews who fuck)
                                                    to provoke

in neon, still useful
in the rain,
          to provoke
some meaning, where before
there was only hell. I said
silence, at his huddled blood.

It is an obscene invention.
A white sticky discharge.
"Jism," in white chalk
on the back of Angel's garage.
Red jackets with the head of
Hobbes staring into space. "Jasm"
the name the leader took, had it
stenciled on his chest.

                      And he sits

wet at the crossroads, remembering distinctly
each weightless face that eases by. (Sun at
the back door, and that hideous mindless grin.

                      (Hear?

Joseph To His Brothers

They characterize
their lives, and I
fill up
with mine. Fill up
with what I have, with what
I see (or
need. I make
no distinction. As blind men
cannot love too quiet beauty.

These philosophers
rein up
their boats. Bring
their gifts, weapons
to my door. As if
that, in itself,
was courage, or counting
science.

The story is a long one. Why
I am here like this. Why you
should listen, now, so late, and
weary at the night. Its
heavy rain
pushing
the grass flat.

It is here
somewhere. It grows
here. Answers. Questions. Noise
as stiff as silence. Silver quiet
beaten heavy under rains. So little
of this we remember. So few portions
of our lives, go on.

Short Speech to My Friends

A political art, let it be
tenderness, low strings the fingers
touch, or the width of autumn
climbing wider avenues, among the virtue
and dignity of knowing what city
you're in, who to talk to, what clothes
—even what buttons—to wear. I address

/ the society
the image, of
common utopia.

/ The perversity
of separation, isolation,
after so many years of trying to enter their kingdoms,
now they suffer in tears, these others, saxophones whining
through the wooden doors of their less than gracious homes.
The poor have become our creators. The black. The thoroughly
ignorant.
          Let the combination of morality
and inhumanity
begin.

2.

Is power, the enemy? (Destroyer
of dawns, cool flesh of valentines, among
the radios, pauses, drunks
of the 19th century. I see it,

as any man's single history. All the possible heroes
dead from heat exhaustion
                    at the beach
                    or hiding for years from cameras
only to die cheaply in the pages
of our daily lie.
              One hero
has pretensions toward literature
one toward the cultivation of errors, arrogance,
and constantly changing disguises, as trucker, boxer,
valet, barkeep, in the aging taverns of memory. Making love
to those speedy heroines of masturbation or kicking literal evil
continually down filmy public stairs.

A compromise
would be silence. To shut up, even such risk
as the proper placement
of verbs and nouns. To freeze the spit
in mid-air, as it aims itself
at some valiant intellectual's face.

There would be someone
who would understand, for whatever
fancy reason. Dead, lying, Roi, as your children
came up, would also rise. As George Armstrong Custer
these 100 years, has never made
a mistake.

The Politics of Rich Painters

is something like the rest
of our doubt, whatever slow thought
comes to rest, beneath the silence
of starving talk.
                    Just their fingers' prints
staining the cold glass, is sufficient
for commerce, and a proper ruling on
humanity. You know the pity
of democracy, that we must sit here
and listen to how he made his money.
Tho the catalogue of his possible ignorance
roars and extends through the room
like fire. "Love," becomes the pass,
the word taken intimately to combat
all the uses of language. So that learning
itself falls into disrepute.

2

What they have gathered into themselves
in that short mean trip from mother's iron tit
to those faggot handmaidens of the french whore
who wades slowly in the narrows, waving her burnt out
torch. There are movies, and we have opinions. There are
regions of compromise so attractive, we daily long
to filthy our minds with their fame. And all the songs
of our handsome generation fall clanging like stones

in the empty darkness of their heads.
                                        Couples, so beautiful
in the newspapers, marauders of cheap sentiment. So much taste
so little understanding, except some up and coming queer explain
cinema and politics while drowning a cigarette.

3

They are more ignorant than the poor
tho they pride themselves with that accent. And
move easily in fake robes of egalitarianism. Meaning,
I will fuck you even if you don't like art. And are wounded
that you call their italian memories petit bourgeois.
                                        Whose death
will be Malraux's? Or the names Senghor, Price, Baldwin
whispered across the same dramatic pancakes, to let each eyelash flutter
at the news of their horrible deaths. It is a cheap game
to patronize the dead, unless their deaths be accountable
to your own understanding. Which be nothing nothing
if not bank statements and serene trips to our ominous countryside.
Nothing, if not whining talk about handsome white men. Nothing
if not false glamourous and static. Except, I admit, your lives
are hideously real.

4

The source of their art crumbles into legitimate history.
The whimpering pigment of a decadent economy, slashed into life
as Yeats' mad girl plummeting over the nut house wall, her broken
knee caps rattling in the weather, reminding us of lands
our antennae do not reach.

And there are people in these savage geographies
use your name in other contexts
think, perhaps, the title of your latest painting
another name for liar.

A Poem For Democrats

the city rises

           in color, our sad
ness, blanket this wood place, single drop
of rain, blue image of
someone's love.
             Net of rain. Crystal ice
glass strings, smash
(on such repertoire of memory
as:
    baskets
    the long walk up harbor
    & the insistence, rain, as they build

City, is wicked. Not
this one, where I am, where they
still move, go to, out of
(transporting your loved one
across the line is death
by drowning.

           Drowned love
hanged man, swung, cement on his feet.)
                          But
the small filth of the small mind
short structures of
newark, baltimore, cincinnati, omaha. Distress,
europe has passed we are alone. Europe
frail woman dead, we are alone

The Measure of Memory
(The Navigator

The presence of good
is its answer (at the curb
the dead white verb, horse
breathing white steam
in the air)
         Leaving, into the clocks
sad lovely lady fixed by words
her man
her rest
her fingers
her wooden house
set against the rocks
of our nation's
enterprise.

That we disappear
to dance, and dance
when we do,
badly.

And wield sentiment
like flesh
like the dumb man's voice
like the cold environment
of need. Or despair, a trumpet
with poison mouthpiece, blind player,
at the garden of least discernment; I

stagger, and remember / my own terrible
blankness and lies.

─────────────

The boat's prow angled at the sun
Stiff foam and an invisible cargo
of captains. I buy injury, and decide
the nature of silence. Lines of speed
decay in my voice.

Footnote To A Pretentious Book

Who am I to love
so deeply? As against
a heavy darkness, pressed
against my eyes. Wetting
my face, a constant trembling
rain.

    A long life, to you. My friend. I
tell that to myself, slowly, sucking
my lip. A silence of motives / empties
the day of meaning.
                What is intimate
enough? What is
beautiful?

       It is slow unto meaning for
any life. If I am an animal, there
is proof of my living. The fawns
and calves
of my age. But it is steel that falls
as a thin mist into my consciousness. As a fine
ugly spray, I have made
some futile ethic
with.

    "Changed my life?" As the dead man
pacing at the edge of the sea. As
the lips, closed

for so long, at the sight
of motionless
birds.
     There is no one to entrust with
meaning. (These sails go by, these small
deadly animals.)
                And meaning? These words?
Were there some blue expanse
of world. Some other
flesh, resting
at the roof
of the world . . .
          you could say of me,
that I was truly
simpleminded.

Rhythm & Blues (1

(for Robert Williams, in exile)

The symbols hang limply
in the street. A forest of objects,
motives,
>   black steaming christ
>   meat wood and cars
>   flesh light and stars
>   scream each new dawn for

whatever leaves pushed from gentle lips
fire shouted from the loins of history
immense dream of each silence grown to punctuation
against the grey flowers of the world.

    I live against them, and hear them, and move
the way they move. Hanged against the night, so many
leaves, not even moving. The women scream tombs
and give the nights a dignity. For his heels
dragged in the brush. For his lips dry as brown wood. As
the simple motion of flesh whipping the air.

An incorrigible motive.
An action so secret it creates.
Men dancing on a beach.
Disappeared laughter erupting as the sea
erupts.
Controlled eyes seeing now all
there is

Ears that have grown
to hold their new maps
Enemies that grow
in silence
Empty white fingers
against the keys (a drunken foolish stupor
to kill these men
and scream "Economics," my God, "Economics"
for all the screaming women drunker still, laid out to rest
under the tables of nightclubs
under the thin trees of expensive forests
informed of nothing save the stink of their failure
the peacock insolence of zombie regimes
the diaphanous silence of empty churches
the mock solitude of a spastic's art.

                      "Love." My God, (after they
scream "Economics," these shabby personalities
the pederast anarchist chants against millions of
Elk-sundays in towns quieter than his. Lunches. Smells
the sidewalk invents, and the crystal music even dumb niggers
hate. They scream it down. They will not hear your jazz. Or
let me tell of the delicate colors of the flag, the graphic blouse
of the beautiful italian maiden. Afternoon spas
with telephone booths, Butterfingers, grayhaired anonymous trustees.
dying with the afternoon. The people of my life
caressed with a silence that only they understand. Let their sons
make wild sounds of their mothers for your pleasure. Or
drive deep wedges in flesh / screaming birds of mourning, at
their own. The invisible mountains of New Jersey, linger
where I was born And the wind on that stone

2

Street of tinsel, and the jeweled dancers
of Belmont. Stone royalty they tear down
for new buildings where fags invent jellies.

A tub, a slick head, and the pink houses waving
at the night as it approaches. A dead fish truck
full of porters I ran track with, effeminate blues singers, the wealth
of the nation transposed into the ring of my flesh's image. Grand dancers
spray noise and disorder in these old tombs. Liverwurst sandwiches dry
on brown fenced-in lawns, unfinished cathedrals tremble with our
    screams.
Of the dozens, the razor, the cloth, the sheen, all speed adventure locked
in my eyes. I give you now, to love me, if I spare what flesh of yours
is left. If I see past what I feel, and call music simply "Art" and will
not take it to its logical end. For the death by hanging, for
the death by the hooded political murderer, for the old man dead in his
tired factory; election machines chime quietly his fraudulent faith.

For the well that marks the burned stores. For the deadly idiot of compromise
who shrieks compassion, and bids me love my neighbor. Even beyond the
    meaning
of such act as would give all my father's dead ash to fertilize their bilious
land. Such act as would give me legend, "This is the man who saved us
Spared us from the disappearance of the sixteenth note, the destruction
of the scale. This is the man who against the black pits of despairing genius
cried, "Save the Popular Song." For them who pat me in the huddle and
    do not
argue at the plays. For them who finish second and are happy they are
    Chinese,
and need not run those 13 blocks.

I am not moved. I will not move to save them. There is no
"melody." Only the foot stomped, the roaring harmonies of need. The
hand banged on the table, waved in the air. The teeth pushed against
the lip. The face and fingers sweating. "Let me alone," is praise enough
for these musicians.

3

My own mode of conscience. And guilt, always the obvious connection.
They spread you in the sun, and leave you there, one of a kind, who
has no sons to tell this to. The mind so bloated at its own judgment. The
railing consequence of energy given in silence. Ideas whose sole place
is where they form. The language less than the act. The act so far beyond
itself, meaning all forms, all modes, all voices, chanting for safety.

I am deaf and blind and lost and still not again sing your quiet verse. I
    have lost
even the act of poetry, and writhe now for cool horizonless dawn. The
shake and chant, bulled electric motion, figure of what there will be
as it sits beside me waiting to live past my own meekness. My own
light skin. Bull of yellow perfection, imperfectly made, imperfectly
understood, except as it rises against the mountains, like sun
but brighter, like flame but hotter. There will be those
who will tell you it will be beautiful.

Crow Jane

"Crow Jane, Crow Jane, don't hold your head so high,
You realize, baby, you got to lay down and die."
—Mississippi Joe Williams

For Crow Jane
(Mama Death.

For dawn, wind
off the river. Wind
and light, from
the lady's hand. Cold
stuff, placed against
strong man's lips. Young gigolo's
of the 3rd estate. Young ruffians
without no homes. The wealth
is translated, corrected, a
dark process, like thought, tho
it provide a landscape
with golden domes.

                    'Your people
without love.' And life
rots them. Makes a silence
blankness in every space
flesh thought to be. (First light,
is dawn. Cold stuff
to tempt a lover. Old lady
of flaking eyes. Moon lady
of useless thighs.

Crow Jane's Manner.

                    Is some pilgrimage
to thought. Where she goes, in fairness,
"nobody knows." And then, without love,
returns to those wrinkled stomachs
ragged bellies / of young ladies
gone with seed. Crow
will not have. Dead virgin
of the mind's echo. Dead lady
of thinking, back now, without
the creak of memory.
                    Field is yellow. Fils dead
(Me, the last . . . black lip hung
in dawn's gray wind. The last,
for love, a taker, took my kin.

Crow. Crow. Where
you leave my
other boys?

Crow Jane in High Society.

                        (Wipes
her nose
on the draperies. Spills drinks
fondles another man's
life. She is looking
for alternatives. Openings
where she can lay all
this greasy talk
on somebody. Me, once. Now
I am her teller.
                (And I tell
her symbols, as the grey movement
of clouds. Leave
grey movements
of clouds. Leave, always,
more.

Where is she? That she
moves without light. Even
in our halls. Even with
our laughter, lies, dead drunk
in a slouch hat famous king.
                        Where?

To come on so.

Crow Jane the Crook.

Of the night
of the rain, she
reigned, reined, her
fat whores and horse.

(A cloud burst,
and wet us. The mountain
split, and burned us. We thought
we were done.

        Jane.
Wet lady of no image. We
thought, you had left us. Dark
lady, of constant promise. We thought
you had gone.

2.

My heart is cast in bitter
metal. Condiments, spices
all the frustration of earth,
that has so much more desire

than resolution. Want than pleasure.
Oh, Jane. (Her boat bumps at the ragged
shore. Soul of the ocean, go out, return.
Oh, Jane, we thought you had gone.

The Dead Lady Canonized.

                          (A thread
of meaning. Meaning light. The quick
response. To breath, or the virgins
sick odor against the night.

                          (A trail
of objects. Dead nouns, rotted faces
propose the nights image. Erect
for that lady, a grave of her own.

                          (The stem
of the morning, sets itself, on
each window (of thought, where it
goes. The lady is dead, may the Gods,

                          (those others
beg our forgiveness. And Damballah, kind father,
sew up
her bleeding hole.

Duncan Spoke of a Process

And what I have learned
of it, to repeat, repeated
as a day will repeat
its color, the tired sounds
run off its bones. In me, a balance.

Before that, what came easiest. From
wide poles, across the greenest earth,
eyes locked on, where they could live, and
whatever came from there, where the hand
could be offered, like Gideon's young troops
on their knees at the water.

                                I test myself,
with memory. A live bloody skeleton. Hung as softly
as summer. Sways like words' melody, as ugly as any
lips, or fingers stroking lakes, or flesh like a
white frightened scream.

What comes, closest, is
closest. Moving, there
is a wreck of spirit,
                        a heap of broken feeling. What

was only love
or in those cold rooms,
opinion. Still, it made
color. And filled me

as no one will. As, even
I cannot fill
myself.

       I see what I love most and will not
leave what futile lies
I have. I am where there
is nothing, save myself. And go out to
what is most beautiful. What some noncombatant Greek
or soft Italian prince
would sing, "Noble Friends."
                      Noble Selves. And which one
is truly
to rule here? And
what country is this?

Audubon, Drafted

(for Linda)

It does not happen. That love, removes
itself. (I am leaving, Goodbye!
                                        Removes
itself, as rain, hard iron rain
comes down, then stops. All those
eyes opened for morning, close with
what few hours given them. With tears,
or at a stone wall, shadows drag down.

I am what I think I am. You are what
I think you are. The world is the
one thing, that will not move. It is
made of stone, round, and very ugly.

If Into Love the Image Burdens

The front of the head
is the scarred cranium. The daisy
night, alone with its mills. Grumbling
through history, with its nest
of sorrow. I felt lost
and alone. The windows
sat on the street and smoked
in dangling winter. To autumn
from spring, summer's questions
paths, present to the head
and fingers. The shelf. The
rainbow. Cold knuckles rub against
a window. The rug. The flame. A woman
kneels against the sill. Each figure
halves silence. Each equation
sprinkles light.

Grey hats and eyes
for the photographed
trees. Grey stones and limbs
and a herd of me's.

Past, perfect.

Each correct color
not in nature, makes
us weep. Each inexpressible
idea. The fog lifts. The fog

lifts. Now falls. The fog
falls.

And nothing is done, or complete. No person
loved, or made better or beautiful. Came here
lied to, leave
the same. Dead boned talk
of history. Grandfathers skid
down a ramp of the night. Flame
for his talk, if it twists
like light on leaves.

Out past the fingers.
Out past the eyes.

Black Dada Nihilismus

.   Against what light

is false what breath
sucked, for deadness.
                    Murder, the cleansed

purpose, frail, against
God, if they bring him
                    bleeding, I would not

forgive, or even call him
black dada nihilismus.

The protestant love, wide windows,
color blocked to Mondrian, and the
ugly silent deaths of jews under

the surgeon's knife. (To awake on
69th street with money and a hip
nose. Black dada nihilismus, for

the umbrella'd jesus. Trilby intrigue
movie house presidents sticky the floor.
B.D.N., for the secret men, Hermes, the

blacker art. Thievery (ahh, they return
those secret gold killers. Inquisitors

of the cocktail hour. Trismegistus, have

them, in their transmutation, from stone
to bleeding pearl, from lead to burning
looting, dead Moctezuma, find the West

a grey hideous space.

2

From Sartre, a white man, it gave
the last breath. And we beg him die,
before he is killed. Plastique, we

do not have, only thin heroic blades.
The razor. Our flail against them, why
you carry knives? Or brutaled lumps of

heart? Why you stay, where they can
reach? Why you sit, or stand, or walk
in this place, a window on a dark

warehouse. Where the minds packed in
straw. New homes, these towers, for those
lacking money or art. A cult of death,

need of the simple striking arm under
the streetlamp. The cutters, from under
their rented earth. Come up, black dada

nihilismus. Rape the white girls. Rape
their fathers. Cut the mothers' throats.

Black dada nihilismus, choke my friends

in their bedrooms with their drinks spilling
and restless for tilting hips or dark liver
lips sucking splinters from the master's thigh.

Black scream
and chant, scream,
and dull, un
earthly
hollering. Dada, bilious
what ugliness, learned
in the dome, colored holy
shit (i call them sinned

or lost
   burned masters
      of the lost
         nihil German killers
            all our learned

art, 'member
what you said
money, God, power,
a moral code, so cruel
it destroyed Byzantium, Tenochtitlan, Commanch
          (got it, *Baby!*

For tambo, willie best, dubois, patrice, mantan, the
bronze buckaroos.

    For Jack Johnson, asbestos, tonto, buckwheat,
    billie holiday.

For tom russ, l'overture, vesey, beau jack,

(may a lost god damballah, rest or save us
against the murders we intend
against his lost white children
black dada nihilismus

A Guerrilla Handbook

In the palm
the seed
is burned up
in the wind.
          In their rightness
the tree trunks are socialists
leaves murder the silence and are brown
and old when they blow to the sea.
                    Convinced
of the lyric. Convinced
of the man's image (since
he will not look at substance
other than his ego. Flowers, grapes
the shadows of weeds, as the weather
is colder, and women walk
with their heads down.
               Silent political rain
against the speech
of friends. (We love them
trapped in life, knowing no way out
except description. Or black soil
floating in the arm.
              We must convince the living
              that the dead
              cannot sing.

Green Lantern's Solo

A deep echo, of open fear: the field drawn in
as if to close, and die, in the old man's eyes
as if to shut itself, as the withered mouth of
righteousness beats its gums on the cooling day.

As if to die
without knowing life.
Having lived, when
he did (an old stout God
in the spent bones
of his dignity. No screams
break his wooden lips
His urine scatters
as steel, which will fall
on any soft thing
you have. (Murder

is speaking of us.

I break and run, or hang back and hide
having been killed by wild beasts in my young wife's
sleep. Having been torn into small echoes of lie, or surrounded
in dim rooms by the smelly ghosts of wounded intellectuals. Old
    science majors
                    whose mothers were brilliant understudys
                or the famous mistress of a benevolent gangster.
    Some mysterious comment on the world at the birth
of the word. Some mysterious jangle of intellects bent on the
    crudeness

of any death so perfectly ignorant as ours.
My friend, the lyric poet,
who has never had an orgasm. My friend,
the social critic, who has never known society,
or read the great italian liars, except his father
who calls the whitehouse nightly, asking for hideous assignments.
My friend who has thrown himself against the dignity of all human flesh
yet beats at its image, as if he was the slow intellect who thought up
God.

No, Nigger, no, blind drunk in SantaSurreal's beard. Dead hero
for our time who would advance the nation's economy by poking holes
in his arms. As golden arms build a forest of loves, and find only
the heavy belly breath of ladies whispering their false pregnancies through
    the
phone. The stagnant image of bats sailing out of their mouths as they
shape the syllable of revenge. Let me say it is Love, but never feeling.
It is knowledge, but never perfection, or something as stupidly callous
as beauty.

2

So important a silence as their lives, dwindled, rusted, corrupted
away. As the port, where smoke rises for the poor french sailor
and his indian whore. There are bones, which still clog those blue
soft seas, and give a human history to nature. Can you understand
that nothing is free! Even the floating strangeness of the poet's head
the crafted visions of the intellect, *named, controlled,* beat and erected
to work, and struggle under the heavy fingers of art. What valley, what
mountain, what eagle or afternoon, is not fixed or changed under our feet
or eyes? What man unremoved from his meat's source, can continue
to believe totally in himself? Or on the littered sidewalks of his personal
history, can continue to believe in his own dignity or intelligence.

Except the totally ignorant
who are our leaders.

        Except the completely devious
        who are our lovers.

                No man except a charlatan
                could be called "Teacher," as

big birds will run off from their young
if they follow too closely, or the drowned youths at puberty
who did not allow that ritual was stronger than
their mother's breasts.

The completely free are the completely innocent, of which
no thing I know can claim: despite the dirty feet
of our wise men, their calm words hung in a line, from city
to city: despite the sickening courage or useless honesty
of men who claim to love each other and resolve their lives
as four letter words: despite the rightness, the strength
the brilliance and character, the undeniable idiocy of poets
like Marx and Rousseau.

                What we have created, is ourselves
                as heroes, as lovers, as disgustingly
                evil. As Dialogues with the soul, with
                the self, Selves, screaming furiously
                to each other. As the same fingers
                touch the same faces, as the same
                mouths close on each other. The killed
                is the killer, the loved the lover
and the islands of mankind have grown huge to include all life,
all lust, all commerce and beauty. Each idea a reflection of itself
and all the ideas men have ever had. Truth, Lie, so close they defy
inspection, and are built into autonomy by naive fools,
who have no wish for wholeness or strength. Who can not but yearn

for the One Mind, or Right, or call it some God, a thing beyond
themselves, some thing toward which all life is fixed, some static,
irreducible, constantly correcting, dogmatic economy

of the soul.

War Poem

The battle waxed (battle wax, good night!
        Steep tumors of the sea's energy
        shells, shells, gold lights under the tree's
        cover.)

                In spring the days explode
                In spain old cuckolds watch their wives
                and send their money to America.

                Straw roofs, birds, any thing we have not
                got. Destroyed before it got here. *Battle,*
                an old dead flower she put on her breast.

                Shells crush the beach. Are crushed
                beneath her feet. Wait for night,
                and the one soldier will not mind us
                sitting here, listening to the familiar
                water, scatter in the shadows.

Political Poem

(for Basil)

Luxury, then, is a way of
being ignorant, comfortably
An approach to the open market
of least information. Where theories
can thrive, under heavy tarpaulins
without being cracked by ideas.

(I have not seen the earth for years
and think now possibly "dirt" is
negative, positive, but clearly
social. I cannot plant a seed, cannot
recognize the root with clearer dent
than indifference. Though I eat
and shit as a natural man (Getting up
from the desk to secure a turkey sandwich
and answer the phone: the poem undone
undone by my station, by my station,
and the bad words of Newark.) Raised up
to the breech, we seek to fill for this
crumbling century. The darkness of love,
in whose sweating memory all error is forced.

Undone by the logic of any specific death. (Old gentlemen
who still follow fires, tho are quieter
and less punctual. It is a polite truth
we are left with. Who are you? What are you
saying? Something to be dealt with, as easily.

The noxious game of reason, saying, "No, No,
you cannot feel," like my dead lecturer
lamenting thru gipsies his fast suicide.

Snake Eyes

That force is lost
which shaped me, spent
in its image, battered, an old brown thing
swept off the streets
where it sucked its
gentle living.
                    And what is meat
to do, that is driven to its end
by words? The frailest gestures
grown like skirts around breathing.
                                        We take
unholy risks to prove
we are what we cannot be. For instance,

I am not even crazy.

A Poem for Speculative Hipsters

He had got, finally,
to the forest
of motives. There were no
owls, or hunters. No Connie Chatterleys
resting beautifully
on their backs, having casually
brought socialism
to England.
       Only ideas,
and their opposites.
          Like,
    he was *really*
    nowhere.

Dichtung

A torn body, correspondent

of extreme cold. Altitude
or thought, colliding as an image
of
moving water, time, the slip

of simple life. It is matter, after all,
that is corrupted, not
spirit. After all, it is spirit
that is corrupted
not matter.
             The role given,
mashed into protein
grace. A lifted arm
in shadow. A lifted thinking
banging silently
in the darkness.
             I fondle what
I find
of myself. Of you
what I understand.
             Trumpets of slow weather.
             Love blends
             in season.

Valéry As Dictator

Sad. And it comes
tomorrow. Again, gray, the streaks
of work
shedding the stone
of the pavement, dissolving
with the idea
of singular endeavor. Herds, the
herds
of suffering intelligences
bunched,
and out of
hearing. Though the day
come to us
       in waves,
              sun, air, the beat
of the clock.
         Though I stare at the radical
world,
     wishing it would stand still.
                Tell me,
and I gain at the telling.
Of the lie, and the waking
against the heavy breathing
of new light, dawn, shattering
the naive cluck
of feeling
       What is tomorrow
that it cannot come
         today?

The Liar

What I thought was love
in me, I find a thousand instances
as fear. (Of the tree's shadow
winding around the chair, a distant music
of frozen birds rattling
in the cold.
    Where ever I go to claim
my flesh, there are entrances
of spirit. And even its comforts
are hideous uses I strain
to understand.
    Though I am a man
who is loud
on the birth
of his ways. Publicly redefining
each change in my soul, as if I had predicted
them,
  and profited, biblically, even tho
  their chanting weight,
      erased familiarity
      from my face.
        A question I think,
an answer, whatever sits
counting the minutes
till you die.

   When they say, "It is Roi
   who is dead?" I wonder
   who will they mean?

BLACK MAGIC

Three Modes of History and Culture

Chalk mark sex of the nation, on walls we drummers
know
as cathedrals. Cathedra, in a churning meat milk.

Women glide through looking for telephones. Maps
weep
and are mothers and their daughters listening to

music teachers. From heavy beginnings. Plantations,
learning
America, as speech, and a common emptiness. Songs knocking

inside old women's faces. Knocking through cardboard trunks.
Trains
leaning north, catching hellfire in windows, passing through

the first ignoble cities of missouri, to illinois, and the panting
Chicago.
And then all ways, we go where flesh is cheap. Where factories

sit open, burning the chiefs. Make your way! Up through fog and
history
Make your way, and swing the general, that it come flash open

and spill the innards of that sweet thing we heard, and gave theory
to.
Breech, bridge, and reach, to where all talk is energy. And there's

enough, for anything singular. All our lean prophets and rhythms.
Entire
we arrive and set up shacks, hole cards, Western hearts at the edge

of saying. Thriving to balance the meanness of particular skies.
Race
of madmen and giants.

Brick songs. Shoe songs. Chants of open weariness.
Knife wiggle early evenings of the wet mouth. Tongue
dance midnight, any season shakes our house. Don't
tear my clothes! To doubt the balance of misery
ripping meat hug shuffle fuck. The Party of Insane
Hope. I've come from there too. Where the dead told lies
about clever social justice. Burning coffins voted
and staggered through cold white streets listening
to Willkie or Wallace or Dewey through the dead face
of Lincoln. Come from there, and belched it out.

I think about a time when I will be relaxed.
When flames and non-specific passion wear themselves
away. And my eyes and hands and mind can turn
and soften, and my songs will be softer
and lightly weight the air.

A Poem Welcoming Jonas Mekas to America

This night's first star, hung
high up over a factory. From my window,
a smile held my poetry in. A tower, where I work
and drink, vomit, and spoil myself for casual life.

Looking past things, to their meanings. All the pretensions
of consciousness. Looking out, or in, the precise stare
of painful reference. (Saying to the pretty girl, "Pain
has to be educational.") Or so I thought, riding down

in the capsule, call it elevator lady, speedless forceless
profile thrust toward the modern lamp, in lieu of a natural
sun. Our beings are here. (Take this chance to lick yourself,
the salt and stain of memory history and object.) Shit! Love!

Things we must have some use for. Old niggers in time on the
dreary street. Man, 50 . . . woman, 50, drunk and falling in the street.
I could say, looking at their lot, a poet has just made a note of your
hurt. First star, high over the factory. I could say, if I had any courage

but my own. First star, high over the factory. Get up off the ground, or
just look at it, calmly, where you are.

A Poem Some People Will Have to Understand

Dull unwashed windows of eyes
and buildings of industry. What
industry do I practice? A slick
colored boy, 12 miles from his
home. I practice no industry.
I am no longer a credit
to my race. I read a little,
scratch against silence slow spring
afternoons.
               I had thought, before, some years ago
that I'd come to the end of my life.
               Watercolor ego. Without the preciseness
a violent man could propose.
               But the wheel, and the wheels,
wont let us alone. All the fantasy
               and justice, and dry charcoal winters
All the pitifully intelligent citizens
               I've forced myself to love.

               We have awaited the coming of a natural
               phenomenon. Mystics and romantics, knowledgeable
               workers
               of the land.

               But none has come.
               (*Repeat*)
                              but none has come.

Will the machinegunners please step forward?

Letter to E. Franklin Frazier

Those days when it was all right
to be a criminal, or die, a postman's son,
full of hallways and garbage, behind the hotdog store
or in the parking lots of the beautiful beer factory.

Those days I rose through the smoke of chilling Saturdays
hiding my eyes from the shine boys, my mouth and my flesh
from their sisters. I walked quickly and always alone
watching the cheap city like I thought it would swell
and explode, and only my crooked breath could put it together
again.

By the projects and small banks of my time. Counting my steps
on tar or new pavement, following the sun like a park. I imagined
a life, that was realer than speech, or the city's anonymous
fish markets. Shuddering at dusk, with a mile or so up the hill

to get home. who did you love
then, Mussolini? What were you thinking,
Lady Day? A literal riddle of image
was me, and my smell was a continent
of familiar poetry. Walking the long way,
always the long way, and up the steep hill.

Those days like one drawn-out song, monotonously
promising. The quick step, the watchful march march,
All were leading here, to this room, where memory
stifles the present. And the future, my man, is long
time gone.

The People Burning

May-Day! May-Day!
　　　　　　　—Pilot talk

They now gonna make us shut up. Ease
thru windows in eight dollar hats
sharpening their pencils on match books. List
our errors and lies, stumbling over our souls
in the dark, for the sake of unnatural advantage.

They now gonna line you up, ask you about God. Nail
your answers on the wall, for the bowling alley owners
to decide. They now gonna pretend they flowers. Snake stalked
large named vegetables, who have, if nothing else,
the title: World's Vilest Living Things.

The Dusty Hearts of Texas, whose most honest world
is the long look into darkness, sensing the glittering
affront of reason or faith or learning. Preferring
fake tiger smells rubbed on the balls, and clothes
the peasants of no country on earth would ever be
vulgar enough to wear. The legacy of diseased mediocrity.

Become an Italian or Jew. Forget the hatred of natural
insolence. The teetering sense of right, as balance, each
natural man must have. Become a Jew, and join the union,
forget about Russia or any radicalism past a hooked grin.
Become an Italian quietist in some thin veneer of reasonable
gain. Lodi, Metuchen, Valley Stream, welcomes you into its
leather ridiculousness. Forget about any anarchy except the

understandable urge to be violent, or flashy, or fast, or
heavy fisted. Sing at Radio City, but never rage at the chosen,
for they have given you the keys to their hearts. Made you
the Fridays and Saturdays of the regime, clothed you in promise
and utility, and banned your thinkers to worship the rags
of your decline.

For the Reconstruction, for the march into any anonymous America,
stretches beyond hills of newsprint, and dishonorable intention.
Forget any dignity, but that that is easily purchased. And recognized
by Episcopalians as they pay their garbage bills. The blueprint's sound.

And the nation is smaller and the loudest mouths are recognized
and stunned by the filth of their hopeless truths. (I've got to
figure this all out. Got to remember just where I came in. Freedom Suite,
some five six years ago, Rollins cradling the sun, as it rose, and we
dreamed then, of becoming, unlike our fathers, and the other cowboys,
strong men in our time, raging and clawing, at fools of any persuasion.)

Now they ask me to be a jew or italian, and turn from the moment
disappearing into the shaking clock of treasonable safety, like reruns
of films, with sacred coon stars. To retreat, and replay; throw my mind out,
sit down and brood about the anachronistic God, they will tell you
is real. Sit down and forget it. Lean on your silence, breathing
the dark. Forget your whole life, pop your fingers in a closed room,
hopped-up witch doctor for the cowards of a recent generation. It is
choice, now, like a philosophy problem. It is choice, now, and
the weight is specific and personal. It is not an emotional decision.
There are facts, and who was it said, that this is a scientific century.

Death Is Not As Natural
As You Fags Seem To Think

I hunt
the black puritan.
                    (Half-screamer

in dull tones
of another forest.

Respecter of power. That it transform, and enlarge
Hierarchy crawls over earth (change exalting space
Dried mud to mountain, cape and whip, swirled
Walkers, and riders and flyers.
Language spread into darkness. Be Vowel
                                        and value
                            Consonant
                                        and direction.
Rather the lust of the thing
than across to droop at its energies. In melted snows
the leather cracks, and pure men claw at their bodies.
Women laugh delicately, delicately rubbing their thighs.

And the dead king laughs, looking out the hole
in his tomb. Seeing the poor
singing his evil songs.

The Success

Among things with souls, find me.
                              Picking thru the alphabet
                         or leaning out the window. (Lives
                    and magic.) Old witch city, the
               lights and roads (floating) up near the tops
        of buildings. Electric names, which are not
    love's. A rolling Eastern distress. Water cutting
    the coast, lulling the mysterious classes.

    Murderers humming under the window.

    A strutting long headed Negro. Beneath the red silk

of unique social fantasy. Shore invisible under tenements.

    The Jew who torments Hitler in Paradise, wiping thick fingers

on a hospital cloth. His fingerprints on the dough, marking it

before baking. Drifting to sleep in Pelham, fucking a female spy.

This man was used against me,
in a dream.
                    Broken teeth
                    Dirty apron
                    Hires a bowery desperado,
                                   to pull out the garbage

      and imagine the whiteness
      of his wife's withered stomach.

    —

Ding

    —

    The proportion of Magic
has seeped so low.

    For the 1st person plural

    America, then,
            Atlantis,
                 in blind overdose.

The New World

The sun is folding, cars stall and rise
beyond the window. The workmen leave
the street to the bums and painters' wives
pushing their babies home. Those who realize
how fitful and indecent consciousness is
stare solemnly out on the emptying street.
The mourners and soft singers. The liars,
and seekers after ridiculous righteousness. All
my doubles, and friends, whose mistakes cannot
be duplicated by machines, and this is all of our
arrogance. Being broke or broken, dribbling
at the eyes. Wasted lyricists, and men
who have seen their dreams come true, only seconds
after they knew those dreams to be horrible conceits
and plastic fantasies of gesture and extension,
shoulders, hair and tongues distributing misinformation
about the nature of understanding. No one is that simple
or priggish, to be alone out of spite and grown strong
in its practice, mystics in two-pants suits. Our style,
and discipline, controlling the method of knowledge.
Beatniks, like Bohemians, go calmly out of style. And boys
are dying in Mexico, who did not get the word.
The lateness of their fabrication: mark their holes
with filthy needles. The lust of the world. This will not
be news. The simple damning lust,

> float flat magic in low changing
> evenings. Shiver your hands
> in dance. Empty all of me for

knowing, and will the danger
of identification,

Let me sit and go blind in my dreaming
and be that dream in purpose and device.

A fantasy of defeat, a strong strong man
older, but no wiser than the defect of love.

The Burning General

Smoke seeping from my veins. Loss from
the eyes. Seeing winter throw its wind
around. Hoping for more, than I'll ever
have. Forgetting my projects, and the projected
sense of order, any claim to "sense" must make.
The reason Allen and the others (even freakish
pseudo dada mama) in the money jungle of controlled
pederasty
                finally bolted. Shut and gone, at the same time.

But can we replace the common exchange of experience with stroking
some skinny girl's penis? Is sense to be lost, all of it, so that
we can walk up Mulberry Street without getting beat up in Italian.

Violence and repression. Silly Nigger hatred for the
silk band of misery. They are right, those farty doctors. Perhaps
it is best to ease into kill-heaven than have no heaven at all.
What do you think, Eddie, out there in Idaho shivering against
the silence, the emptiness of straight up America? What's it look like
there?

Can we ask a man to savor the food of oppression? Even
if it's rich and full of mysterious meaning. Can you establish
(and that word must give my whole game away) any kind of equality?
Can there be such thing forced on the world? That is, that the poor
and their owners appreciate light wherever they are, simply as light.
Why are you so sophisticated? You used to piss and shit in your pants.
Now you walk around *thinking* all the time, as if that sacred act

would rewrite the world in bop talk, giving medals to every limping coon
in creation.

Is there more to it than that? This is the time to ask, even while perfecting
your line. We realize that ends and means should be separated, but who
will do the separating? The evaluating. You want your experience
thought of as valuable. Which is, listen baby, only another kind
of journalistic enterprise. Not worthy of that bumpy madness
crawled up your thighs when the urine dried those sweet lost winters,
and tears were the whole fucking world.

Tone Poem

(for Elvin Jones and Bob Thompson)

A host of loves is the city, and its memory
dead sense traveling (from England) on the sea
for two hundred years. The travelers show up in Japan
to promote peace and prosperity, perhaps a piece
of that nation's ass. Years later, years later,
plays rework the rime of lust. As history, and a cloud
their faces bang invisible notes, wind scribbled leaves
and foam. An eagle hangs above them spinning. Years and travelers
linger among the dead, no reports, gunshots white puffs
deciding the season and the mode of compromise. The general good
has no troops or armor, subtly the books stand closed, except
sad facts circled for unknown hippies carrying the mail.
I leave it there, for them, full of hope, and hurt. All the poems
are full of it. Shit and hope, and history. Read this line
young colored or white and know I felt the twist of dividing
memory. Blood spoiled in the air, caked and anonymous. Arms opening,
opened last night, we sat up howling and kissing. Men who loved
each other. Will that be understood? That we could, and still
move under cold nights with clenched fists. Swing these losers
by the tail. Got drunk then high, then sick, then quiet. But thinking
(and of you lovely shorties sit in libraries seeking such ideas out).
I'm here now, LeRoi, who tried to say something long for you. Keep it.
Forget me, or what I say, but not the tone, and exit image. No points,
or theories, from now on, just me and mine, when they get me, just
think of me as typing with a drink at my right hand, some women who
love me . . . and the day growing old and sloppy through the window.

Gatsby's Theory of Aesthetics

Verse, as a form, is artificial. Poetry is not a form, but rather a result. What-
ever the matter, its meaning, if precise enough in its information (and
direction) of the world, is poetic. The poetic is the value of poetry, and any
concatenation of elements is sufficient to induce the poetic. What you see
is as valuable as what you do not. But it is not as meaningful (to you).
Poetry aims at difficult meanings. Meanings not already catered to. Poetry
aims at reviving, say, a sense of meaning, or meaning's possibility and ubiq-
uitousness.

Identification can be one term of that possibility. That is, showing a
thing with its meaning apparent through the act of that showing. Inter-
pretation can be another term. That is, supporting a meaning, with one's
own life. That is, under, standing. And using that position as a map, or dic-
tionary. Depending on whether you move or sit.

I write poetry only to enlist the poetic consistently as apt description of
my life. I write poetry only in order to feel, and that, finally, sensually, all
the terms of my life. I write poetry to investigate my self, and my meaning
and meanings.

But also to invest the world with a clearer understanding of it self, but
only by virtue of my having brought some clearer understanding of my self
into it. I wrote in a poem once, "Feeling predicts intelligence."

But it is possible to feel with any part of our consciousness. Whatever
part of us does register: whatever. The head feels. The heart feels. The penis
feels. The penis is also, because it is able to feel, conscious, and has intelli-
gence of its own. No one can deny that intelligence, or at least no one
should try. The point of life is that it is arbitrary, except in its basest forms.
Arbitrariness, or self imposed meaning, is the only thing worth living for.
It is the only thing that permits us to live.

The only time I am conscious of my limitations is when I am writing. The rest of the time, there is no standard, at all reasonable, for judging, in fact, what limitations are.

Year of the Buffalo
1964

All's Well

(For E.R. & M.B.)

African in the Bush of the Hatreds. One gone.

An old time love withered, in seeing, off and on
in a thing like rain (the wetness in your head, and
all the stampeding, fear, hacked open skulls grinning
sensing your loss, the words floating just beyond your
fingers (invisible antennae

Just drew a blank, dope nod
corrupting what's left, and that nothing
confusion of blankness, the hatred when I wake
silence for motives, she, woman I am with, is
silent, as the dream of some other woman, never
existed, tho she be of flesh and red sperm spinning
through her veins. This woman came when I stuck her
iron insect screams holes. Blood flew up into the
dropper, we sent it back in her. Eyes rolled up,
lap quivered, lip shook. The next time she
got depressed going cross town. She held me so.
Not understanding the buildings stopped, and sky
hung above them just the same

The Bronze Buckaroo

for Herb Jeffries

Soft night comes back
with its clangs and dreams. Back
in through the base
of the hairy skull. The heavy pictures, unavailable
solaces, emptying their churchy magic
out. Golden girls, and thin black ones
patrol the dreamer's meat. Things
shovel themselves, from where they always are. Spinning, a
moment's indecision, past the vision of stealth and silence
Byron thought the night could be. Death blow Eliot silence, dwindling
away, in the 20th century. Poet clocks crouched in their Americas.
Dreaming of poems, only the cold sky could bring. Not room poems, or
fireplace poems, or the great washed poetry of our dizzy middleclass.
But something creeps and grabs them, rapes them on the pavement. The
    Screams
are not essays, rich blonde poetess from the mysteries of Kipling's harmon
nica! Not guileful treatises of waste and desire, stuck somewhere
nursing her tilted beauty, like some old fashion whore, embarrassed
by God, or his diseases. The funny heart blows smoke, in the winter
and gives us all the earth we need. In summer, it sweats, and remembers.
Half way up the hill the mutineers stand, and seek their comrades out.
I am half way up, and standing.

Numbers, Letters

If you're not home, where
are you? Where'd you go? What
were you doing when gone? When
you come back, better make it good.
What was you doing down there, freakin' off
with white women, hangin' out
with Queens, say it straight to be
understood straight, put it flat and real
in the street where the sun comes and the
moon comes and the cold wind in winter
waters your eyes. Say what you mean, dig
it out put it down, and be strong
about it.

I cant say who I am
unless you agree I'm real

I cant be anything I'm not
Except these words pretend
to life not yet explained,
so here's some feeling for you
see how you like it, what it
reveals, and that's Me.

Unless you agree I'm real
that I can feel
whatever beats hardest
at our black souls

I am real, and I can't say who
I am. Ask me if I know, I'll say
yes, I might say no. Still, ask.
I'm Everett LeRoi Jones, 30 yrs old.

A black nigger in the universe. A long breath singer,
wouldbe dancer, strong from years of fantasy
and study. All this time then, for what's happening
now. All that spilling of white ether, clocks in ghostheads
lips drying and rewet, eyes opening and shut, mouths churning.

I am a meditative man, And when I say something it's all of me
saying, and all the things that make me, have formed me, colored me
this brilliant reddish night. I will say nothing that I feel is
lie, or unproven by the same ghostclocks, by the same riders
always move so fast with the word slung over their backs or
in saddlebags, charging down Chinese roads. I carry some words,
some feeling, some life in me. My heart is large as my mind
this is a messenger calling, over here, over here, open your eyes
and your ears and your souls; today is the history we must learn
to desire. There is no guilt in love.

Red Eye

(for Calvin Hernton and Ishmael Reed)

The corrupt madness of the individual. You cannot live
alone. You are in the world. World, fuck them. World rise
and twist like you do, night madness in rain as heavy as stones.
Alabama gypsy talk, for peeling lips. Look in your mother's head,
if you really want to know everything. Your sister's locked up
pussy. Invasion of the idea syndrome like hand clapping winter in.
Winter will make you move. Or you will freeze in Russia and
never live to see Napoleon as conceived by Marlon Brando.
We are at the point where death is too good for us. We are
in love with the virtue of evil. This communication. Rapping
on wet meat windows, they spin in your head, if I kill you
will not even have chance to hate me

A Western Lady

The sick tightening. Brain damage movie
of forbidden flesh, laying in the shadows
breathing without purpose, meat stacked
in terrible silence, her mother wept
to think of that meat, her father, paced
and said the star spangled banner into
his brain damage soup. These were windows
we looked through. The brother died in a
guitar school, stringing guitars and praying
for a piece. And it was his own movie star
slipping green panties over high heels. Hence
his pimples, and the bunching of his waistband.
No one is expected to be rich *and* smart. Hence
planes go down from 30,000, full of screaming
materialists, whose mothers stunted them
hanging around election machines. It was the metal clack
that did it. A flag lobotomy, which has the victims
wallowing on warehouse floors, whistling popular Bach.
I suffer with these announcers. Butter and egg men,
whose promise rolled with the big ice, them's pre-
historic times.

Return of the Native

Harlem is vicious
modernism. BangClash.
Vicious the way its made.
Can you stand such beauty?
So violent and transforming.
The trees blink naked, being
so few. The women stare
and are in love with them
selves. The sky sits awake
over us. Screaming
at us. No rain.
Sun, hot cleaning sun
drives us under it.

The place, and place
meant of
black people. Their heavy Egypt.
(Weird word!) Their minds, mine,
the black hope mine. In Time.
We slide along in pain or too
happy. So much love
for us. All over, so much of
what we need. Can you sing
yourself, your life, your place
on the warm planet earth.
And look at the stones

the hearts, the gentle hum
of meaning. Each thing, life
we have, or love, is meant
for us in a world like this.
Where we may see ourselves
all the time. And suffer
in joy, that our lives
are so familiar.

Black Art

Poems are bullshit unless they are
teeth or trees or lemons piled
on a step. Or black ladies dying
of men leaving nickel hearts
beating them down. Fuck poems
and they are useful, wd they shoot
come at you, love what you are,
breathe like wrestlers, or shudder
strangely after pissing. We want live
words of the hip world live flesh &
coursing blood. Hearts Brains
Souls splintering fire. We want poems
like fists beating niggers out of Jocks
or dagger poems in the slimy bellies
of the owner-jews. Black poems to
smear on girdlemamma mulatto bitches
whose brains are red jelly stuck
between 'lizabeth taylor's toes. Stinking
Whores! We want "poems that kill."
Assassin poems, Poems that shoot
guns. Poems that wrestle cops into alleys
and take their weapons leaving them dead
with tongues pulled out and sent to Ireland. Knockoff
poems for dope selling wops or slick halfwhite
politicians Airplane poems, rrrrrrrrrrrrrrrr
rrrrrrrrrrrrrrr . . . tuhtuhtuhtuhtuhtuhtuhtuhtuh
. . . rrrrrrrrrrrrrrrr . . . Setting fire and death to
whities ass. Look at the Liberal

Spokesman for the jews clutch his throat
& puke himself into eternity . . . rrrrrrrr
There's a negroleader pinned to
a bar stool in Sardi's eyeballs melting
in hot flame Another negroleader
on the steps of the white house one
kneeling between the sheriff's thighs
negotiating cooly for his people.
Agggh . . . stumbles across the room . . .
Put it on him, poem. Strip him naked
to the world! Another bad poem cracking
steel knuckles in a jewlady's mouth
Poem scream poison gas on beasts in green berets
Clean out the world for virtue and love,
Let there be no love poems written
until love can exist freely and
cleanly. Let Black People understand
that they are the lovers and the sons
of lovers and warriors and sons
of warriors Are poems & poets &
all the loveliness here in the world

We want a black poem. And a
Black World.
Let the world be a Black Poem
And Let All Black People Speak This Poem
Silently
or LOUD

Poem for HalfWhite College Students

Who are you, listening to me, who are you
listening to yourself? Are you white or
black or does that have anything to do
with it? Can you pop your fingers to no
music, except those wild monkies go on
in your head, can you jerk, to no melody,
except finger poppers get it together
when you turn from starchecking to checking
yourself. How do you sound, your words, are they
yours? The ghost you see in the mirror, is it really
you, can you swear you are not an imitation greyboy,
can you look right next to you in that chair, and swear,
that the sister you have your hand on is not really
so full of Elizabeth Taylor, Richard Burton is
coming out of her ears. You may even have to be Richard
with a white shirt and face, and four million negroes
think you cute, you may have to be Elizabeth Taylor, old lady,
if you want to sit up in your crazy spot dreaming about dresses,
and the sway of certain porters' hips. Check yourself, learn who it is
speaking, when you make some ultrasophisticated point, check yourself,
when you find yourself gesturing like Steve McQueen, check it out, ask
in your black heart who it is you are, and is that image black or white,

you might be surprised right out the window, whistling dixie on the way in.

American Ecstasy

"Loss of Life or Both Feet or Both Hands or Both Eyes . . . . The Principal Sum

Loss of One Hand and One Foot . . . . The Principal Sum

Loss of One Hand and One Eye or One Foot and One Eye . . . . .The Principal Sum

Loss of One Hand or One Foot . . . . One half The Principal Sum

Loss of One Eye . . . . One fourth The Principal Sum"

Are Their Blues Singers In Russia?

Spies are found wanting. They wanted
in line, on the snow, a love to get high
with, and not, the line, a lie, a circling
tone of merciless involvement, the pushing, the
stomping, an image of green space was what the spy
wanted, standing there being shoved and hurled around
by his nostrils. They cold nights, after waiting, and
worse mornings. When the girls go by, and the lights go off
and on, to forget the clocks, and the counting of cobblestones
to keep pure cellar static off his back. The li'l darling, holding
'is wee wee he gotta pee, a little run down he leg. He pants soiled,
the wind freezed that part of his leg that wanted love most

We stand for tragic emblems when we return to the pros and cons
of the world. The shielding, for nothing. God's contradictions we
speak about as if we knew something, or could feel past what we
describe, and enter the new forms of being. See the door and enter,
get in out of the snow, the watermoccasins, and stuff, mud he
carried around in his mouth, or on the ground up to his ankles,
it'll get stupid or boring. So much, so much, to prepare a proper
place, to not exist in.

The day was a bargain.
A jew on the corner was thinking
of bargains. A dog, out back
did not start yet, howling, puny words,
barking in sorrow, a boat, for the spy's family to ride in
while they watched a sinking image of the world, and the spy's death

in snow they could really dig as beautiful or cool or somewhere else,
or just grimy lace curtains would make them hang against the boat's window
dreaming of God. The disappointment would come
after they opened their mouths, or version last
would come, and coparmies would salute the jewish dog
barking the rhythms of embezzled deserts.

We are all spies for god.

We can get betrayed. We ask for it, we ask
so much. And expect the fire the sun set the horizon
to slide through human speech dancing our future dimensions.
We expect some real shit. We expect to love all the things
somebody runs down to us. We want things, and are locked here, to the earth,
by pussy chains, or money chains, or personal indulgence chains, lies, weak
phone calls, attempts to fly when we know good and fucking well we can't
    and even
the nerve to get mad, and walk around pretending we are huge magnets
    for the
most beautiful force in the universe. And we are, but not in the image of
    wind
spreading the grass, or brown grass dying from a sudden snow, near the
    unemploy-
ment office where the spy stands trying to remember just why he wanted to
be the kinda spy he was

HARD FACTS

History On Wheels

Civil Rights
included Nathan
and the rest
of them, who got in america
big shotting off the agony
a class of blue Bloods, hip
to the swing and sway of
the usa. yeh all the 1st
negroes world wide, joined
knees, and shuffled heroically
into congress, city hall, the
anti-p program, and a thousand
penetrable traps of cookstove
america. a class of exploiters,
in black face, collaborators,
not puppets, pulling their own
strings, and ours too, in the
poor people's buck dance, w/o
the bux. But see, then later,
you talkin afrika, and its unity
like a giant fist of iron, smashing
"racialism," around the world. But see
that fist, any fist, reared back to
strike an enemy, shd strike the real
enemy. Not a colorless shadow for
black militants in residence, to
bloat the pockets and consolidate
the power of an international

bourgeoisie. In rag time, slanting
stick legs, with a pocket full of
toasted seaweed, and a bibliography
of bitter neocapitalists or bohemian
greys, celebrating life in a dark garage
w/ all cars banned until the voodoo car
appear. The way the rich blackies showed
after we marched and built their material
base, now niggers are left in the middle
of the panafrikan highway, babbling about
eternal racism, and divine white supremacy
a hundred thousand dollar a year oppression
and now the intellectualization, the militant
resource of the new class, its historical
valorization. Between them, john johnson
and elijah, david rockefeller rests his
smiling head.

Das Kapital

Strangling women in the suburban bush
they bodies laid around rotting while martinis are drunk
the commuters looking for their new yorkers feel a draft
& can get even drunker watching the teevee later on the Ford
replay. There will be streams of them coming, getting off
near where the girls got killed. Two of them strangled by
the maniac.
There are maniacs hidden everywhere cant you see? By the dozens
and double dozens, maniacs by the carload (tho they are
a minority). But they terrorize us uniformly, all over the place
we look at the walls of our houses, the garbage cans parked full
strewn around our defaulting cities, and we cd get scared. A rat
eases past us on his way to a banquet, can you hear the cheers raised
through the walls, full of rat humor. Blasts of fire, some woman's son will
    stumble
and dies with a pool of blood around his head. But it wont be the maniac.
    These old houses
crumble, the unemployed stumble by us straining, ashy fingered, harassed.
    The air is cold
winter heaps above us consolidating itself in degrees. We need a aspirin or
    something, and
pull our jackets close. The baldhead man on the television set goes on in a
    wooden way
his unappetizing ignorance can not be stood, or understood. The people
    turn the channel
looking for Good Times and get a negro with a pulldown hat. Flashes of
    maniac shadows before
bed, before you pull down the shade you can see the leaves being blown

down the street
too dark now to see the writing on them, the dates, and amounts we owe.
  The streets too
will soon be empty, after the church goers go on home having been saved
  again from the
Maniac . . . except a closeup of the chief mystic's face rolling down to his
  hands will send
shivers through you, looking for traces of the maniacs life. Even there among
  the mythophrenics.

What can you do? It's time finally to go to bed. The shadows close around
  and the room is still.
Most of us know there's a maniac loose. Our lives a jumble of frustrations
  and unfilled
capacities. The dead girls, the rats noise, the flashing somber lights, the dead
  voice on
television, was that blood and hair beneath the preacher's fingernails? A few
  other clues

we mull them over as we go to sleep, the skeletons of dollarbills, traces of
  dead used up
labor, lead away from the death scene until we remember a quiet fit that
  everywhere
is the death scene. Tomorrow you got to hit it sighs through us like the
  wind, we got to
hit it, like an old song at radio city, working for the yanqui dollarrrr, when
  we were
children, and then we used to think it was not the wind, but the maniac
  scratching against
our windows. Who is the maniac, and why everywhere at the same time . . .

Real Life

Ted, Ted? In the bay at the bottom of the wat
er lies the president of the united states,
his chappaqui
dick, bent around an immigrant in an
automobile. Nixon calls from the coast, you thought
you'd get away clean, but my vengeance
comes from beyond the grave.
Nixon slobbers on the phone, wetting the cocaine on the desk
he and pat have been snorting since
early morning, herb alpert blurting low contradictions in the wings
Shadows gather on the windows, then blow twisted into the whole dark
which comes now he lights go on
in the white house. Ford cracking his knuckles
turns off the tv and calls nixon
you alright dick, he says, white whistles jag at nixons calm, high
and wild, pat's jaws quivering, green and blues come off the screen
and stutter 3-D in the room, sympathetic and wanting to rub them
he cant speak
rockefeller's talking
ford says the plan, was national
unity, the new money
and the old,
he cant speak, nixon cant, high, and hot, cripple forever upstairs
pat starts to pee on the rug, and roll in it. Her giggles like a vincent
price movie, without popcorn, nixon slobbers, trying to make a point, ford
is saying national unity, as rockefeller grins, his finger, shoving up into
the air, across a thousand miles, at the mad western capitalists and their
southern friends. Yall dont know how, this shit works, he is saying (really)

the commentator, looks over his shoulder, as if he knows that nixon is
watching. Ford whispers numbly, dick, dick, yes,
mr. president?

Horatio Alger Uses Scag

Kissinger has made it, yall. He's the secretary
of state, U.S.A. The anglo-snakes have called him
mooing to their side, his bag-time with rocky helped
a lot. His ol lady, was once, they say, rocky's main
squeeze . . . intellectually. But Henry, the k, pushes through
his dangerous glasses. His wine smile sloshes back and forth
he's thinking, as he speaks. A fast man on his feet. The subject,
a cold threat to the a-rabs (it makes him feel vaguely nationalistic,
but not in an irresponsible way, him bein a jew and all
ya know . . . but they hired him not for his jewishness "grrr . . . he sd
what is that", but for his absolute mastery of the art of
bullshitting.
And so, he lays it all out
across the U.N. decks for all
to hear, and be afraid. His freckles, even,
show, so synonomous with america is this
fat priapic mackman
A-rabs, he says, you betta
be cool with that oil & shit
& beyond us all, you cdda laught
is the realization that the shadowy figure
in the arab getup, is yo man, rocky, makin
the whole thing
perfect

When We'll Worship Jesus

We'll worship Jesus
When jesus do
Somethin
When jesus blow up
the white house
or blast nixon down
when jesus turn out congress
or bust general motors to
yard bird motors
jesus we'll worship jesus
when jesus get down
when jesus get out his yellow lincoln
w/the built in cross stain glass
window & box w/black peoples
enemies we'll worship jesus when
he get bad enough to at least scare
somebody—cops not afraid
of jesus
pushers not afraid
of jesus, capitalists racists
imperialists not afraid
of jesus shit they makin money
off jesus
we'll worship jesus when mao
do, when toure does
when the cross replaces Nkrumah's
star
Jesus need to hurt some a our

enemies, then we'll check him
out, all that screaming and hollering
& wallering and moaning talkin bout
jesus, jesus, in a red
check velvet vine + 8 in. heels
jesus pinky finger
got a goose egg ruby
which actual bleeds
jesus at the apollo
doin splits and helpin
nixon trick niggers
jesus w/his one eyed self
tongue kissing johnny carson
up the behind
jesus need to be busted
jesus need to be thrown down and whipped
till something better happen
jesus aint did nothin for us
but kept us turned toward the
sky (him and his boy allah
too, need to be checkd
out!)
we'll worship jesus
when he get a boat load of ak-47s
and some dynamite
and blow up abernathy robotin
for gulf
jesus need to be busted
we ain't gonna worship nobody
but niggers gettin up off
the ground
not gon worship jesus
unless he just a tricked up

nigger somebody named
outside his race
need to worship yo self fo
you worship jesus
need to bust jesus (+ check
out his spooky brother
allah while you heavy
on the case
cause we ain gon worship jesus
we aint gon worship
jesus
we aint gon worship
jesus
not till he do somethin
not till he help us
not till the world get changed
and he ain, jesus ain, he cant change the world
we can change the world
we can struggle against the forces of backwardness, we can
   change the world
we can struggle against our selves, our slowness, our connection
   with
     the oppressor, the very cultural aggression which binds us to
       our enemies
     as their slaves.
we can change the world
we aint gonna worship jesus cause jesus dont exist
xcept in song and story except in ritual and dance, except in
   slum stained
tears or trillion dollar opulence stretching back in history, the
   history
of the oppression of the human mind
we worship the strength in us

we worship our selves
we worship the light in us
we worship the warmth in us
we worship the world
we worship the love in us
we worship our selves
we worship nature
we worship ourselves
we worship the life in us, and science, and knowledge, and
    transformation
of the visible world
but we aint gonna worship no jesus
we aint gonna legitimize the witches and devils and spooks and
    hobgoblins
the sensuous lies of the rulers to keep us chained to fantasy and
    illusion
sing about life, not jesus
sing about revolution, not no jesus
stop singing about jesus,
sing about, creation, our creation, the life of the world and
    fantastic
nature how we struggle to transform it, but dont victimize our
    selves by
distorting the world
stop moanin about jesus, stop sweatin and crying and stompin
    and dyin for jesus
unless thats the name of the army we building to force the land
    finally to
change hands. And lets not call that jesus, get a quick
    consensus, on that,
lets damn sure not call that black fire muscle
    no invisible psychic dungeon
no gentle vision strait jacket, lets call that peoples army, or

wapenduzi or
    simba
wachanga, but we not gon call it jesus, and not gon worship
    jesus, throw
jesus out yr mind. Build the new world out of reality, and new
    vision
we come to find out what there is of the world
to understand what there is here in the world!
to visualize change, and force it.
we worship revolution

A New Reality Is Better Than a New Movie!

How will it go, crumbling earthquake, towering inferno, jugger-
  naut, volcano, smashup,
in reality, other than the feverish nearreal fantasy of the capitalist
  flunky film hacks
tho they sense its reality breathing a quake inferno scar on their
  throat even snorts of
100% pure cocaine cant cancel the cold cut of impending death
  to this society. On all the
screens of america, the joint blows up every hour and a half for
  two dollars an fifty cents.
They have taken the niggers out to lunch, for a minute, made us
  partners nigger Charlie) or
surrogates (boss nigger) for their horror. But just as superafrikan
  mobutu cannot leop
  ardskinhat his
way out of responsibility for lumumba's death, nor even with his
  incredible billions
  rockefeller
cannot even save his pale ho's titties in the crushing weight of
things as they really are.
How will it go, does it reach you, getting up, sitting on the side
of the bed, getting ready to go to work. Hypnotized by the ma-
chine, and the cement floor, the jungle treachery of
  trying
to survive with no money in a money world, of making the boss
100,000 for every 200
  dollars
you get, and then having his brother get you for the rent, and if

163

you want to buy the car
    you
helped build, your downpayment paid for it, the rest goes to buy
his old lady a foam
    rubber
rhinestone set of boobies for special occasions when kissinger
drunkenly fumbles with her blouse, forgetting himself.
If you don't like it, what you gonna do about it. That was the
question we asked each
    other, &
still right regularly need to ask. You don't like it? Whatcha
gonna do, about it??
The real terror of nature is humanity enraged, the true
technicolor spectacle that
    hollywood
cant record. They cant even show you how you look when you
go to work, or when you
    come back.
They cant even show you thinking or demanding the new so-
cialist reality, its the ultimate
    tidal
wave. When all over the planet, men and women, with heat in
their hands, demand that
    society
be planned to include the lives and self determination of all the
people ever to live. That is the scalding scenario with a cast of
just under two billion that they dare not even whisper. Its called,
"We Want It All . . . The Whole World!"

A Poem for Deep Thinkers

Skymen coming down out the clouds land
and then walking into society try to find out
whats happening—"Whats happening," they be saying
look at it, where they been, dabbling in mist, appearing &
disappearing, now there's a real world breathing—inhaling
exhaling concrete & sand, and they want to know what's
happening. What's happening is life itself "onward & upward,"
the spirals of fireconflict clash of opposing forces, the dialogue of
yes and no, showed itself in stabbed children in the hallways of
schools, old men strangling bankguards, a hard puertorican
inmate's

   tears

exchanging goodbyes in the prison doorway, armies sweeping
wave after wave to contest the ancient rule of the minority. What
draws them down, their blood entangled with

   humans,

their memories, perhaps, of the earth, and what they thought it
could be. But blinded by sun, and their own images of things,
rather than things as they actually are, they wobble, they
stumble, sometimes, and people they be cheering alot, cause
they think the skymen dancing, "Yeh . . . Yeh . . . get on
it. . . . ," people grinning and feeling good cause the

   skymen

dancing, and the skymen stumbling, till they get the sun out
they eyes, and integrate the inhead movie show, with the
material reality that exists with and without them. There are
tragedies, tho, a buncha skies bought the loopdieloop program
from the elegant babble of the ancient minorities. Which is

where they loopdieloop in the sky right on just
   loopdieloop
in fantastic meaningless curlicues which delight the thin gallery
owners who wave at them on their way to getting stabbed in the
front seats of their silver alfa romeos by lumpen they have gotten
passionate with. And the loopdieloopers go on, sometimes
spelling out complex primitive slogans and shooting symbolic
smoke out their gills in honor of
   something
dead. And then they'll make daring dives right down toward the
earth and skag cocaine
   money
whiteout and crunch iced into the statue graveyard where Ralph
Ellison sits biting his
   banjo
strings retightening his instrument for the millionth time before
playing the star spangled banjo. Or else loopdieloop loopdieloop
up higher and higher and thinner and thinner and
   finer
refiner, sugarladdies in the last days of the locust, sucking they
greek lolliepops.
Such intellectuals as we is baby, we need to deal in the real
world, and be be in the real world. We need to use, to use, all
the all the skills all the spills and thrills that we conjure, that we
construct, that we lay out and put together, to create life as
beautiful as we thought it could be, as we dreamed it could be,
as we desired it to be, as we knew it could be, before we took
off, before we split for the sky side, not to settle for endless
meaningless circles of celebration of this madness, this madness,
not to settle for this madness this madness madness, these yoyos
yoyos of the ancient minorities. Its all for real, everythings for
real, be for real, song of the skytribe walking the earth, faint
smiles to open roars of joy, meet you on the battlefield they say,

they be humming, hop, then stride, faint smile to roars of open
joy, hey my man, what's happening, meet you on the
    battlefield
they say, meet you on the battlefield they say, what i guess needs
to be discussed here
    tonight
is what side yall gon be on

POETRY FOR THE ADVANCED

Pres Spoke in a Language

Pres
        spoke in a language
"of his own." What did he say, between the
horn line
s, pork pie hat
tenor tilted
pres once was a drummer but gave it up cause other dudes
        was getting
the foxes
while he packed his tomtoms
"Ding Dong," pres sd, meaning
like a typewriter, its the end
of this
line. "No Eyes," pres wd say, meaning
I didn't cdn't dig it, and what it was was
lame. Pres
had a language
and a life, like,
all his own,
but in the teeming whole of us he lived
toooting on his sideways horn
translating frankie trumbauer into
Bird's feathers
Tranes sinewy tracks
the slickster walking through the crowd
surviving on a terrifying wit
its the jungle the jungle the jungle
we living in

and cats like pres cd make it because they were clear they, at
  least,
had to,
to do anything else.
Save all that comrades, we need it.

REGGAE OR NOT!

Reggae or Not!

A piece to be read with Reggae accompaniment.

Inside beyond our craziness is reality. People rushing through life
dripping with
funk. Inside beyond our craziness and the lies of phillistines
who never wanted to be anything
but Bootsie
w/ golden curls
and a dress tho they black as tar
beyond our inside, beyond wvo, beyond craziness
dripping with
reality
is the funk
the real fusion of life and life
heart and history
color and motion grim what have you's
beat us eat us send us into flight
on the bottom-ism on the bottom
up under-ism, up under
way down-ism way down under-ville
feet bottoms, everybody put us down
we down
how we got down
how we got, hot, how we got so black
& blue
how we cd blow
how we cd know
how we cd, and did, and is, and bees, how
how how, and how how how, and how and why and why why

like big eye nigger motion
heavywt champ
white hope party
populists in hoods
the real jesse jackson
our history
our pain
our flight
our fright
our terror . . . AHEEESSSSHHHHHHHHEEEEEEEEEEEEEEEEEE
our women watched when the crackers cut off our balls
in the grass, they made the little girls watch
stuffed them in our mouths
(this was before they complained about
OPEC, before they complained about baraka being rude
before malcolm set kenneth clark on fire
(and after too . . .
            but history
               the development of the afroamerican nation
            in the black belt south.

from blue slaves
from green africa
from drum past and pyramid hipness
from colors colors all the time, everyday, bright—bright—brightness
   red green yellow purple orange wearing niggersssss AAAAAAHHHHHH
violet violent shiny head shiny shoe knife carryin niggerssssssss
                    AAAAAAAAA
            dust, cripples staggering
              white hats, blood, blood in the cotton
          wear the fuck out it
         love you baby
         drunk motherfucker

preachin in the twilight madness and jesus fuckem
hell all around
white face hell
   inside beyond the madness history
beyond the scag, history
beyond the oppression and exploitation
                            Aheeeeeeeeeee—balls
                                   in the sand

     preach!!
   baldhead rip off
       teach!!
    chicken eatin metaphysical
      loud talkin chained up motherfuckas
    anykinda nigger jet plane flyin ishmael reed lyin nigger
andy young hung like a sign announcing the new policy
  get a paycheck pay the madness pay the blood pay the history
    beyond the sick ness and racism
    history
today's combustion
   for the revolutionary future
     beyond the madness and cocaine
    beyond the male chauvinism and baby actin niggers
   who want disco to substitute for their humanity & struggle
And the alligators clappin they hands Garvey, man
       yeh, Nat man, alligators in the sunlight
       in the day time now
         sittin beside us groundin
   man, I see it
    it no fool I
  I no be fool dem tink
   no fool I
alligators Marcus
  Nat man, they come right up to us

and explain scientific why our shit aint right
why we need to be under dem,
why we need to bend and sway like
dead boy wilkie, downtown with them
no fool I, I no for fool, bee, bee crazy sometime
sometime be out, be way out,
like crazy mother fucka
purple language come out I mouth
ya know,
but Nat man,
Marcus,
alligator
they organize to love us
take us out ourselves
got whip mout whip eye whip talk
all for fool I but I no be no fool for they
I no go for ghost, like dig, pig, I fuck you up for fun

like a dance
like pussy russo in the joint
want to control the pills
instead the blood drove a shank in his titty
ya punk he scream they take him into solitary
an alligator
he say why you want to separate bozo
((that he inside name for I
bozo, like H.Box Brown say, the muthafucka
upsidedown
he bozo
I—I
all eyes, a we eye, us, like raging black purpleness
as music, as rhythmic sun screams our color lay for them

The nation, he said,
he had been cut,
the nation
does not, he said,

      and before he cd get it out
      I drove the blade deep down thru
      the adam's apple, severing the jugular

      and man, hey, instead a blood
      ya know, the racist punk,
      all words spill out
        all words run on ground like bleach waterbug
    all words say no, like lula, say no, say, like lula, no
   say, hey, say, no, like lula, trying to kill i i no like clay
  say he, words spill out where blood shd be, abstract shit all out
  say hey, why you gonna split

        1979 a calm time compared
      1979 cool compared to what will be
    1979 fire in me banked compared
  up against what will be
all I's we, this cant go on
this cant go on, all this
this craziness, beyond it is us
    is history, our lives, and
    the future. Beyond this
    beyond craziness, beyond capitalism
    beyond national oppression and racism
    beyond the subjugation of women
    disco bandit style beyond
    lies of the disco bandit
    beyond lies of the mozart freaks
    beyond joe papap and papap joe

beyond breznev, and all the little multi-colored breznev clones
masquerading as radicals telling persons they revolutionaries
beyond all the little latest generation of human failure pettybourgeois
explainers of the bullshit, beyond everything but what will last what is
real, what the people will make and demand, what they are and have been,
there is Self Determination and Revolution
There is Revolution and Self Determination
there is the fire so broad a rainbow of fire, a world full of fire
there is all bullshit for now exploding
so ready all busshit for next be explode
all fire so flame rise so for fire be heavy and everywhere now

Self Determination
& Revolution   (sing)
Revolution
& Self Determination

World, to be, for I and that person
and every person, for all I's all we's all they's all all's together be
cool now compared to explosion life future
when every minute is blow up of everyting stupid always
is cool now compared to all exploded jack the ripper rich ass
to people smashed powerful garbage dead forever by our hand
to destroyed dumb systems of exploited pain corrected by annihilation only
forever till the next shit
be in the struggle conscious comrade
be in the struggle righteous friend
its cool now, the nation, the workers mad but shit aint rose
beyond the calmness history and pain
beyond the torture history and future fill each other with flame
its cool now, the alligators talking to us like we cant see whats on they mind
jimmy carter cant talk to you
jesse jackson cant talk to you
bootsie and the funkadelic cant talk to you
Who can talk to you—who can still bullshit you

who can set you up with lies you aint heard
with unscientific science and metaphysical analysis
alligators in the disguise of the hiptime
alligators from the old alligator pad,
fake communists, sham revolutionaries
they can and do and will till broke head screams
talk to you they can shorenuff anyway busshit the besta
you, but a alligator got bad breaff smell like a alligator
a alligator eyes is white and bloodshot, full of alligator
images, a alligator brain is fulla alligator thoughts teethy
and slimy and fulla dead half ate animals. a alligator bite
when they talk and they tryin to con you they be bitin and it
hurt so you bash them and they look at you weird you say stop
bitin muthafucka and talk if you goin to i dont eat no alligator
but they make hip pouches to carry my goddam papers in
It's a higher level of bullshit goin down
a much higher level of bullshit
goin down, aint even bullshit, its alligator shit
some sophisticated amphibian feces goin down
up under they bumps and tears, up under they alligator eyes
mostly up under they alligator
lies. a much higher level of bullshit goin down

do you really think Henry Winston was hipper than Rochester and if so why
do you really think Andy Young was hipper than Andy Old
or that Angela Davis was hipper than Beaulah or Poncho be with Cisco
or that Alligators got sidekicks hipper than Gabby was with Roy & Dale
Some sidekick muthafuckers some sidekicks, want us to call the nation
    sidekickania
got sidekick inside they eyes eat and breathe love bein sidekicks and got
    sidekickitis
so much grey stuff hang out they ears droolin eye tears into dirt
come out the closet sidekicks

its calm now & cool, 1979 a calm time, sidekicks can still get over
ride alligators upriver to trade, the jungle is smokin but coolin
and the sidekick deals get made. Come out the closet sidekick
Roy Rogers retired, Cisco doin reruns
Mantan been canonized by the Sidekick society
And Booker T. been made an official militant on the lower east side

cant tell multinational unity
from side kick-ism-itis might even fight us
but all folk got to dig it for be real
for be hot
for be us
for be life thrown into future
too much pain go down
too much hate
too many people like we, no go for alligator
                                        ghost
        we is nation in suffering
        we is nation in chains
        the latest spears will not even be spears
        tho the warcries sound the same
        reach out for the comrades reach out for true comrades
        reach out for allies reach out for real allies
        no fool I this alligator, all I's look for light
        we no be fool for alligator, nor the alligator big time friend
        We be for heat & fire
        We be for genuine war
        No be fool for alligator
        Self Determination ⎫
        Revolution ⎭ (sing)
        We know our friend for fighting
        We know our comrade for struggle
        no be bullshit only for word noise

no be dry dull stuff but war war war war war
fuck a bourgeois alligator
lyin he tryin to be help
we know our friend for fighting
we see our comrade they struggle
no be fool for alligator
with some new time chauvinistic lie, by, by, by, no fool I
by, no fool all I

dead folks dead pass away
rich shit dead pass away
liars imitating revolution die
pass away
beyond bullshit is history
beyond deadshit is history & pain
niggers riding alligators will get blown away when the alligator do
even in the calmest of times
Self Determination Revolution } (sing)
Revolution Self Determination
We no be fool
for alligator
our comrade hear and understand
To liberate we got kill
To liberate blood must flow
To liberate imperialism gotta go
we for kill racism, we for kill our oppression and every other person
too
alligator bullshit for big time rich folks
he bite yr militance off like sleepy monkey with tail
in the wrong place
its calm now, jojo, story teller, compared to other future time hotting
hotting be back be back be black be black and all other color too
we for win anyway

we for all us win
we in people laughing our victory song
our victory
song go like this

Self Determination
Revolution
Self Determination
Revolution   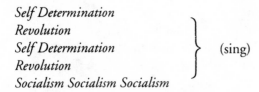   (sing)
Self Determination
Revolution
Self Determination
Revolution
Socialism Socialism Socialism
DEATH TO ALLIGATOR EATING CAPITALISM
DEATH TO BIG TEETH BLOOD DRIPPING IMPERIALISM
I be black angry communist
I be part of rising black nation
I be together with all fighters who fight imperialism
I be together in a party with warmakers for the people
I be black and african and still contemporary marxist warrior
I be connected to people by blood and history and pain and struggle
We be together as party as one fist and voice
We be I be We, We We, the whole fist and invincible flame
We be a party soon, we know our comrade for struggle
We be war to come we bring war we no go for alligator
we kill his trainer too

Self Determination
Revolution
Self Determination   (sing)
Revolution
Socialism Socialism Socialism

Only Socialism will save
the Black Nation
Only Socialism
will save the Black Nation
Only Socialism will save
America
Only Socialism will save
the world!

AM/TRAK

1

Trane,
Trane,
History Love Scream Oh
Trane, Oh
Trane, Oh
Scream History Love
Trane

2

Begin on by a Philly night club
or the basement of a cullut chuhch
walk the bars my man for pay
honk the night lust of money
oh
blow —
scream history love

Rabbit, Cleanhead, Diz
Big Maybelle, Trees in the shining night forest
Oh
blow
love, history

Alcohol we submit to thee
3x's consume our lives
our livers quiver under yr poison hits
eyes roll back in stupidness

The navy, the lord, niggers,
the streets
all converge a shitty symphony
of screams
  to come
  dazzled invective
Honk Honk Honk, "I am here
to love
it". Let me be fire-mystery
air feeder beauty"
Honk
Oh
scream—Miles
comes.

   3

Hip band alright
sum up life in the slick
street part of the
world, oh,
blow,
If you cd
nigger
man

Miles wd stand back and negative check
oh, he dug him—Trane
But Trane clawed at the limits of cool
slandered sanity
with his tryin to be born

raging
shit
    Oh
    blow,
        yeh go do it
        honk, scream
        uhuh yeh—history
                love
                blue clipped moments
                of intense feeling.
"Trane you blows too long".
Screaming niggers drop out yr solos
Bohemian nights, the "heavyweight champ"
smacked him
  in the face
his eyes sagged like a spent
dick, hot vowels escaped the metal clone of his soul
fucking saxophone
tell us shit tell us tell us!

    4

There was nothing left to do but
be where monk cd find him
that crazy
mother fucker
        duh duh-duh duh-duh duh
        duh duh
        duh duh-duh duh-duh duh
        duh duh
        duh duh-duh duh-duh duh
        duh duh

      duh Duuuuuuuuuhhhhhh
Can you play this shit? (Life asks
Come by and listen

& at the 5 Spot Bach, Mulatto ass Beethoven
& even Duke, who has given America its hip tongue
checked
checked
Trane stood and dug
Crazy monk's shit
Street gospel intellectual mystical survival codes
Intellectual street gospel funk modes
Tink a ling put downs of dumb shit
pink pink a cool bam groove note air breath
a why I'm here
a why I aint
& who is you - ha - you - ha - you - ha
Monk's shit
Blue Cooper 5 Spot
was the world busting
on piano bass drums & tenor

This was Coltrane's College. A Ph motherfuckin d
sitting at the feet, elbows
& funny grin
Of Master T Sphere
  too cool to be a genius
he was instead
Theolonius
with Comrades Shadow
on tubs, lyric Wilbur
who hipped us to electric futures
& the monster with the horn.

5

From the endless sessions
money lord hovers oer us
capitalism beats our ass
dope & juice wont change it
Trane, blow, oh scream
yeh, anyway.

There then came down in the ugly streets of us
inside the head & tongue
of us
a man
black blower of the now
The vectors from all sources — slavery, renaissance
bop charlie parker,
nigger absolute super-sane screams against reality
course through him
AS SOUND!
   "Yes, it says
this is now in you screaming
recognize the truth
recognize reality
& even check me (Trane)
who blows it
Yes it says
Yes &
Yes again   Convulsive multi orgasmic
               Art
               Protest

& finally, brother, you took you were

(are we gathered to dig this?
electric wind find us finally
on red records of the history of ourselves)

The cadre came together
the inimitable 4 who blew the pulse of then, exact
The flame the confusion the love of
whatever the fuck there was
    to love
Yes it says
blow, oh honk-scream (bahhhhhhh — wheeeeeeee)

(If Don Lee thinks I am imitating him in this poem,
this is only payback for his imitating me - we
are brothers, even if he is a backward cultural nationalist
motherfucker — Hey man only socialism brought by revolution
can win)

        Trane was the spirit of the 60's
        He was Malcolm X in New Super Bop Fire
        Baaahhhhh
        Wheeeeeee . . . . Black Art! ! !
Love
History
  On The Bar Tops of Philly
in the Monkish College of *Express*
in the cool Grottoes of Miles Davis Funnytimery
Be
Be
Be reality
Be reality alive in motion in flame to change (You Knew It!)
                to change! !
       (All you reactionaries listening

Fuck you, Kill you
get outta here! ! !)

Jimmy Garrison, bass, McCoy Tyner, piano, Captain Marvel Elvin
on drums, the number itself — the precise saying
all of it in it afire aflame talking saying being doing meaning
Meditations,
Expressions
A Love Supreme
(I lay in solitary confinement, July 67
  Tanks rolling thru Newark
  & whistled all I knew of Trane
  my knowledge heartbeat
  & he was *dead*
they
said.
And yet last night I played *Meditations*
& it told me what to do
Live, you crazy mother
fucker!
  Live!
  & organize
  yr shit
  as rightly
  burning!

IN THE TRADITION

In the Tradition

(for Black Arthur Blythe)

*"Not a White Shadow
But Black People
Will be Victorious . . . "*

Blues walk weeps ragtime
Painting slavery
women laid around
working feverishly for slavemaster romeos
as if in ragtime they spill
their origins like chillers   (lost chillen
in the streets to be
telephoned to by Huggie
Bear from channel 7, for the White Shadow
gives advice on how to hold our homes
together, tambien tu, Chicago Hermano)

> genius bennygoodman headmaster
> philanthropist
> romeos —
> but must coach
> cannot shoot —
>
> hey coah-ch
> hey coah-ch
> trembling fate wrapped in flags
> hey coah-ch
> you can hug this

while you at it
coah-ch
Women become
goils gals grinning in the face of his
no light
Men become
boys & slimy roosters crowing negros
in love with dressed up pimp stupidity death
hey coah-ch
wanna outlaw the dunk, cannot deal with skyman darrell
or double dippin hip doctors deadly in flight
cannot deal with Magic or Kareem . . . hey coah-ch coah-ch
bench yrself in the garbagecan of history o new imperial dog
denying with lying images
our strength & African
funky beauty

nomatter the three networks idiot chatter

Arthur Blythe
Says
it!
in the
tradition

2

Tradition
of Douglass
of David Walker
Garnett
Turner
Tubman

        of ragers yeh
          ragers
                 (of Kings, & Counts, & Dukes
                 of Satchelmouths & SunRa's
                 of Bessies & Billies & Sassys
                 & Ma's
        Musical screaming
        Niggers
        yeh
     tradition
        of Brown Welles
        & Brown Sterling
        & Brown Clifford
        of H Rap & H Box

Black baltimore sister blues antislavery singers
        countless funky blind folks
        & oneleg country beboppers
        bottleneck in the guitarneck dudes
        whispering thrashing cakewalking raging
        ladies
        & gents
        getdown folks, elegant as
        skywriting
     tradition
        of DuBois
        Baby Dodds & Lovie
      Austin, Sojourner
      I thought I heard Buddy Bolden

           say, you're terrible
           you're awful, Lester
           why do you want to be

the president of all this
of the blues and slow sideways
horn. tradition of blue presidents
locked up in the brig for wearing zoot suit
army pants. tradition of monks & outside dudes
of marylous and notes hung vibrating blue just beyond just after
just before just faster just slowly twilight crazier than europe or its
racist children

bee-doo dee doop bee-doo dee dooo doop (Arthur
tradition
of shooters
& silver fast dribblers
of real fancy motherfuckers
fancy as birds flight, sunward/high
highhigh
sunward
arcs/swoops/spirals
in the tradition
¼ notes
eighth notes
16th notes
32nds, 64ths, 128ths, silver blue
presidents
of Langston & Langston Manifestos
Tell us again about the negro artist
& the racial mountain so we will not
be negro artists, Mckay Banjoes and
Homes In Harlem, Blue Black Boys &
Little Richard Wrights, Tradition of
For My People Margaret Walker & David Walker & Jr Walker
& Walker Smith Sweet Ray Leonard Rockin in Rhythm w/
Musical Dukes,

What is this tradition Basied on, we Blue Black Wards strugglin
against a Big White Fog, Africa people, our fingerprints are
   everywhere
on you america, our fingerprints are everywhere, Cesaire told
   you
that, our family strewn around the world has made more parts of
   that world
blue and funky, cooler, flashier, hotter, afro-cuban james
   brownier
         a wide panafrican
         world

   Tho we are afro-americans, african americans
let the geographic history of our flaming hatchet motion
                 hot ax motion
                hammer & hatchet

        our cotton history
        our rum & indigo
            sugar cane
          history

Yet, in a casual gesture, if its talk you want, we can say
Cesaire, Damas, Depestre, Romain, Guillen
You want Shaka, Askia, (& Roland Snellings too)
      Mandingo, Nzinga, you want us to drop
        Cleopatra on you or Hannibal
         What are you masochists
          paper iron chemistry
          & smelting
           I aint even mentioned
            Troussaint or Dessaline
            or Robeson or Ngugi

Hah, you bloody & dazed, screaming at me to stop yet,
NO, hah, you think its over, tradition song, tradition
poem, poem for us together, poem for arthur blythe
  who told us again, in the tradition
                      in the
                tradition of

    life & dying
      in the tradition of those klanned & chained
    & lynched and shockleyed and naacped and ralph bunched

hah, you rise a little I mention we also the tradition of amos and
  andy
hypnotized selling us out vernons and hooks and other nigger
  crooks of
gibsons and crouches and other assorted louses of niggers that
  turn from
gold to shit proving dialectics muhammad ali style
But just as you rise up to gloat I scream COLTRANE! STEVIE
  WONDER!
                MALCOLM X!
              ALBERT AYLER!
              THE BLACK ARTS!

Shit & whistling out of my nkrumah, cabral, fanon, sweep—I cry
  Fletcher
Henderson, Cane, What Did I Do To Be So Black & Blue, the
  most perfect
  couplet in the language, I scream Mood Indigo, Black
    Bolshevik, KoKo,
  Now's the Time, Ark of Bones, Lonely Woman, Ghosts, A Love
    Supreme,
  Walkin, Straight No Chaser, In the Tradition

of life
& dying
centuries of beautiful
women
crying
In the tradition
of screamed
ape music
coon hollers
shouts
even more profound
than its gorgeous
sound
In the tradition of
all of us, in an unending everywhere at the same time
line
in motion forever
like the hip Chicago poet Amus Mor
like the Art Ensemble
like Miles's Venus DeMilo
& Horace Silver reminding us
& Art Blakey sending us messages
Black Brown & Beige people
& Pharaoh old and new, Blood Brotherhoods
all over the planet, land songs land poems
land sculptures and paintings, land niggers want still want
will get land
in the tradition of all of us in the positive aspect
all of our positive selves, cut zora neale & me & a buncha other
folks in half. My brothers and sisters in the tradition. Vincent
Smith & Biggers, Color mad dudes, Catlett & White Chas & Wm,
BT, Overstreet
& the 60s muralists. Jake Lawrence & Aaron Douglass & Ademola

Babatunde Building More Stately Mansions
We are the composers, racists & gunbearers
We are the artists
Dont tell me shit about a tradition of deadness & capitulation
of slavemasters sipping tea in the parlor
while we bleed to death in fields
tradition of cc rider
see what you done done
dont tell me shit about the tradition of slavemasters
& henry james I know about it up to my asshole in it
dont tell me shit about bach mozart or even ½ nigger
beethoven
get out of europe
come out of europe if you can
cancel on the english depts this is america
north, this is america
where's yr american music
gwashington won the war
where's yr american culture southernagrarians
   academic aryans
    penwarrens & wilburs
  say something american if you dare
   if you
    can
     where's yr american
     music
      Nigger music?

(Like englishmen talking about *great* britain stop with tongues
 lapped on their cravats you put the irish on em. Say shit
man, you mean irish irish Literature . . . when they say about
 they
you say nay you mean irish irish literature you mean, for the

last century you mean, when you scream say nay, you mean
    yeats,
synge, shaw, wilde, joyce, ocasey, beckett, them is, nay, them is
irish, they's irish, irish as the ira)

you mean nigger music? dont hide in europe—"oh thats
    classical!"
    come to this country
            nigger music?

you better go up in appalachia
and get some mountain some coal mining
songs, you better go down south in our land
& talk to the angloamerican national minority
they can fetch up a song or two, country & western
could save you from looking like saps before the world
otherwise
            Palante!
            Latino, Native American
            Bomba, Plena, Salsa, Rain dance War dance
            Magical invective
            The Latin Tinge
            Cherokee, Sonny Rollins w/Clifford Brown
            Diz & Machito, or Mongo SantaMaria

        Comin Comin World Saxophone Quartet you cannot
stand up against, Hell No I Aint Goin To Afghanistan, Leon
Thomas million year old pygmies you cannot stand up against, nor
Black Arthur tellin you like Blue Turhan Bey, Odessa, Romance can
Bloom even here in White Racist Land It can Bloom as Beautiful,
though flawed by our oppression it can
bloom bloom, in the tradition
        of revolution

Renaissance
Negritude
Blackness
Negrissmo
Indigisme
sounding niggers
swahili speaking niggers niggers in turbans
rna & app & aprp & cap black blacks
& assembly line, turpentine, mighty fine female
blacks, and cooks, truck drivers, coal miners
small farmers, iron steel and hospital workers
in the tradition of us
in the tradition of us
the reality not us the narrow fantasy
in the tradition of african american black people/america

nigger music's almost all
you got, and you find it
much too hot

in the tradition thank you arthur for playing & saying
reminding us how deep how old how black how sweet   how
we is and bees
when we remember
when we are our memory as the projection
of what it is evolving
in struggle
in passion and pain
we become our sweet black
selves

once again,
in the tradition

in the african american
   tradition
      open us
      yet bind us
      let all that is positive
      find
      us
         we go into the future
            carrying a world
               of blackness
                  yet we have been in the world
                  and we have gained all of what there
                  is and was, since the highest expression
                  of the world, is its total

& the universal
is the entire collection
of particulars

ours is one particular
one tradition
of love and suffering truth over lies
and now we find ourselves in chains
   the tradition says plainly to us fight plainly to us
   fight, that's in it, clearly, we are not meant to be slaves
it is a detour we have gone through and about to come out
in the tradition of gorgeous africa blackness
says to us fight, it's all right, you beautiful
   as night, the tradition
thank you langston/arthur
says sing
says fight
in the tradition, always clarifying, always new and centuries old

says
    Sing!
    Fight!
        Sing!
       Fight!
            Sing!
           Fight! &c. &c.
                    Boosheee dooooo doo doooo dee
                      doooo
                    dooooooooooo!
                    DEATH T   O THE KLAN!

HEATHENS

Heathens

(Freedom Jazz Dance or Dr. Jackle)

1   They Ugly
    on purpose!

2   They get high
    off Air Raids!

3   They are the oldest
    continuously functioning
    Serial Killers!

4   They murder
    to Explain
    Themselves!

5   They think
    Humans
    are food.

6   They imitate
    conversation
    by lying

7   They are always naked
    and always dirty
    the shower & tuxedo
    don't help

8   They go to the bathroom
     to have a religious
       experience

9   They believe everything is better
     Dead. And that everything alive
      is their enemy.

10 Plus Heathens is armed
     and dangerous.

Heathens in Evolution

When their brains got
  large enough
They created
  Hell!

Heathen Bliss

To be Alive
& Ignorant

Devil Worship

is Heathen
Self Respect

Civil Rights Bill # 666

The Negro Heathen Enablement Act.

"Essentially, it allows more Negroes to become
Heathens."

Heathen Technology & Media

Seek to modernize
cannibalism

& make it
acceptable to

the food.

"Christ Was Never in Europe!"

(Kwame Toure)

AT LYNCHINGS
HEATHENS WEAR
WHITE TIE
IN FORMAL
HOOD & ROBE

IN THIS FRENZIED
RITUAL
THEY RECONFIRM
THE SUPERIORITY
OF THEIR CULTURE!

Heathens Think Fascism is Civilization

AND THAT THEY ARE SUPERIOR
TO HUMANS & THAT
HUMANITY IS METAPHYSICAL

To under stand that . . .

can you? I mean really
      really dig what that means . . . It's like monsters roaming
the earth . . . who sting to live, who know no better. Who, like
wild animals, might sing, or make a sound some way, that
might pretend, imitate, a human cry, the sweet rationality of
love.

That is the art of it, that it exists and carries with it, so many
complexities, even that craziness, but then aesthetics is con-
nected to the real. The deadliness of that

ugliness, or uncomprehended smoothness. The technology of
predatory creatures who feed on flesh, who shit on the tender
aspirations of human evolution, because they have no concep-
tion of humanity. Except as that natural yelp, which they can
see as somehow, a reflex of what that might be. It took that
kind of vision for them to understand the use of religion in the
changing world. To cloak themselves in the modest trappings
of early christianity, having murdered its prophet for power and
profit.

WISE, WHY'S, Y'S

Wise I

WHYS *(Nobody Knows*
The Trouble I Seen)
Trad.

If you ever find
yourself, some where
lost and surrounded
by enemies
who won't let you
speak in your own language
who destroy your statues
& instruments, who ban
your omm bomm ba boom
then you are in trouble
deep trouble
they ban your
own boom ba boom
you in deep deep
trouble

humph!

probably take you several hundred years
to get
out!

Wise 2

Billie's Bounce
Charlie Parker

I was of people
caught in deep trouble
like I scribe you
some deep trouble, where
enemies had took us
surrounded us / in they
country
then banned our
ommboom ba boom

the confusion
the sickness

   /What vision in the blackness
        of queens
        of kings
                /What vision in the blackness
          that head
        & heart
        of yours

      that sweet verse
      you made, I still hear
      that song, son
       of the son's son's son's
           son

I still hear that
   song,
   that cry
   cries
   screams
life exploded

   our world exploding us
   transformed to niggers

What vision
in the blackness
your own hand sold you
"I am not a king or queen," your own hand
if you bee of the royal catch
or the tribes soulwarped by the ghoulishness

I still hear those songs and cries
of the sons and sons and daughters and daughters
I still bear that weeping in my heart
that bleeding in my memory

And I am not a king
nor trader in flesh
I was
of the sufferers
I am among those
to be avenged!

Wise 3

Hipnosis
Grachan Moncur III

Son singin
fount some
words/ Son
singin
in that other
language
talkin bout "bay
bee, why you
leave me
here," talkin bout
"up unner de sun
cotton in my hand." Son
singing, think he bad
cause he
can speak
they language, talkin bout
"dark was the night
the ocean deep
white eyes cut through me
made me weep."

Son singin
fount some words. Think
he bad. Speak
they
language.

'sawright
I say
'sawright
wit me
look like
yeh, we gon be here
a taste

Wise 4

Dewey's Circle
David Murray

No coat has I got
no extra chop
no soft bed or favor
no connection with the slaver

dark was the night
our eyes had not met
I fastened my life to me
and tried to find my way

talk did I hear
of fires and burning
and death to the gods

on the dirt where I slept
such talk
warmed me

such talk
lit my way

I has never got nothing but hard times and punishment
Any joy I had I made myself, and the dark woman
who took my hand and led me to myself

I has never got nothing
but a head full of blood
my scar, my missing teeth.

I has never got nothing but
killer frustration/ yes dark
was the night
cold was the ground

I has never got nothing, and talk
of rebellion
warmed me

Song to me, was the darkness
in which I could stand
my profile melted into the black air
red from the flame of the burning big house

in those crazy dreams I called myself
Coltrane
bathed in a black and red fire
in those crazy moments I called myself
Thelonius
& this was in the 19th century!

Y's 18

Explainin' The Blues (Ma Rainey)
"Georgia Tom" Dorsey

What are
these
words

to
tell
it

all?

      facts
      acts
      Do they have
      their own
      words?

      !Exacts!

    The Scientist in love
       w/precision
   but we need
    this
   we must have
    it
   the exact real
   the concrete
   what it is

& that whole
is story

Africa
Slave
mind memory
Birth
A land across
       the ocean
Blue Water
Green world
       Blood
& Stopped Motion

These mismatched slaves
they cooled
readjusted
the black
     forever
the white
     till the debt's
     paid
     (for them to
        become
        as new
        as we
        so they
        become
        the overseers)

this world of
     limits
     twists

       & opposing
        forces

these elements
of constant
Change

What is yr world
& yr face
yr clock's
  confession

Have you slept w/
       the constitution
       3/5ths of the darkness
       spoke to

refer to the records
thereby
dumb romance
it's lie
for a flag's
    health
a class
stealth
    to cover
      its murder
      its beatings

As a domestic
    bleeding
    a near by
    tragedy.

We cd go to Dred Scott
    for testimony
    Henry Bibb

We cd ask Linda B
    or Henry
    The Box

We cd be drawn into
    eternity
    w/David and his
    Appeal

To speak of all
    we have
    feel!

Only reality
    say
Where we will
    go
It's tethers
Its' chains
Its' sick pricks
    inventing
    crushings
    for our lives
    a decoration
    of horror
they cd define
    & understand
they cd justify
    our deaths
    & torture

they cd be clean
    & taking
    a little

   taste

As the lightning
tried to illuminate
Animal life

Their smiles even
    chill us
    mad poseur
    posing as
    the mad doctor
    who is the original

    American
    Nazi
The southern Himmlers
& Goebbels, baked
    in our dying

What the war
    proposed
        our entrance
        as citizens
        who once had been
        slaves

This 13, 14 & 15 yr numbers
       in the
       lottery

This Freedman's Bureau
this 40 acres

    as grounds for
    identical
    social
    valence
    political
    economic

       (not Sociology & Social Democratic
            political
            Bohemianism)

Revolution, The question
    the answer

What revolution
    cd not be
      destroyed
        bought
    or postponed?

What revolution
  cd not be
    sold out?

All those
 in the real
    world

all those
  that have

actually
been

The betrayal of Niggers was necessary
to welcome
Imperialism!

That was its condition
The Killing of
Nigger
Democracy

So Spain
it's decorated
past
The Philippines, Puerto Rico
Cuba, the booty

The new era

amidst our sunlight
mass laughter
emancipation
The Paris
Commune

The Berlin meeting to divide
the Dark Places
Colonial Pie

What the Slave Trade
Wrought.

That one day the Heathens
wd actually come on the real
side - that they wd take our
hearts as funny valentines

That they wd stick our lives & history

in the toilet bowl
        (toxic
        waste)

& claim our
     past
& future

As the Commune
      smashed
      dead

   The rehearsals
        for Buchenwald
        & Belsen
carried out in the
        American
        South

Unwilling nigger actors
              Heavy
              Minstrels
          this torture Birth
          of the

     Black Nation

The "rule by naked terror"

can not be called
   Fascism

because we
  are
Niggers

& that
is too
famous
for the likes
of us

Fascism
   wd come later
   in Europe
   (naturally)
   & be well advertised

   as an excuse
   for Israeli
   imperialism

History-Wise #22

Black Mountain Blues
Bessie Smith

"The only
     railroad
          guaranteed
not to break down!"

100 years
     Before
     The Col-
       trane
         The
   real
   sub
   way

                Ms "Moses'" Streamliner
                John Parker's Darker

Sparker
at Night
No light
but a far star
North

&wayoff
Like a whistle or a horn

The black night
fills

our ears

We gon' go
has already

gone

"Choo Choo" is the translation
in somebody else's

Station

#

Whoooooeeee Whoooooeeee
Whoooooooeoooo Whoooooooeeoooo Whooooeeeeoooo

is its real
sound

from way up under
the ground

Way
Down

Whooooweeeee   Whooooeoooooeeooo
Whooooeeeoooooeeeooo

Thats it real
sound
Under Ground!

& then sometimes
if the night is cold
& bright

that whistle cries
like all through

that night

that whistle cries
& it moans

Whyyyyyyyyyyyyyyyyyyyyyyyyyyyyyyyyyyyyyyy'sssssssssss
  Whyyyyyyyyyyyyyyyyyyyyyyyyyyyyyyyyyysssssssssssss
    Whyyyyyyyyyyyyyyyyyyyyyyyyyyyyyyyyyyy
       &c.

1929: Y you ask? (26)

Chime Blues
FletcherHenderson
(piano solo)

In "The Masque of the Red Death"
near the end
of the ball
a deadly stranger appears.
Not Vincent Price,
Some thing with eyes like numbers
mouth a siren about to wail
Screamed headlines, the dope of the radio.
The party goers freeze
the Butlers and Maids get their notices
they are skeleton walkers, boat feet,
Wings, dark countenanced baritones
Willowy sopranos; the hall
Swept with an actual tide
of Red & Black—The White
is the silence as the Flag Waves.

Did some one say, "The Renaissance
is over?" Or was that the living
Dying wind, reality, or the Rags
of yr future? The living dying wind
adhesive against wet w/ blood top hats
souls w/bullet holes. Ex leapers smashed
against the bankruptcy of bullszit & oppression.

Finally we know, half superiorly,
all these guests
will die of the Plague. The Black Death!
The Red Death! The Plague!

Horror movie statistical murders.
Dead in old houses

& under cars. In chain gang Gulags
& share cropper concentration camps.

Most of us wake up in a crumbling
plague ridden mansion.
Imitation music
Imitation laughter
Imitation people
w/ Imitation Lives-
A nation of minstrels
and ignorant powerful people
plus slave niggers almost as insane
as their
oppressors!

A ritual of Black & Red Caped
Devil Messengers
In the shadow of the casement glass

Our glasses, raised in the air,
are frozen
in a shadow
as wet
as blood!

It begins to snow outside
beyond the dead forest,
inside the naked empty grey cities

The snow is spotted w/ blood.
A madman's signature
is shown on television.

Disease, now, is
continuous!

Stellar Nilotic (29)

You Gotta Have Freedom
Pharoah Sanders

You want to know
how I escaped? (There were bright yellow lights now, and red
flashes.)

Can we talk here? Are we all ex-slaves? (a laughter
ruins the dawn silence, and the birds acknowledge us
with their rap of flutes).

That star, just over the grey green peak (the moonlight
acknowledges us and makes us shadows.) Was how I was led,

A slender black woman, around 23, put out her hand, turning
toward the star. You know how night is, the star was blue and
beautiful. Around it music, we drummed through the forests.

Their ignorance, that country of "Their" and its united snakes
unified in madness, and worship of advantage. You cannot
have aristocracy, except you have slaves.

They teach you that.

Yet our going, our breathing, the substance
of our lives, was with us chanting

against whatever was not cool.

This was always, and remains
a foreign land. And we are

undoubtedly, the slaves.

There is some music, that shd come on now.
With space for human drama, there shd be some memory
that leaves you smiling. That is, night and the way/
Her lovely hand, extended. The Star, the star, all night
We loved it
like ourselves.

At The Colonial Y They Are Aesthetically
& Culturally Deprived (Y's Later) (31)

Maple Leaf Rag
Scott Joplin

SHARK MONSTER Rockefeller
          Codes. Explosion is War.
          For Wha? (The Blood)
                    Profits
                    of New
Avant disease   come to ya'
What was in the bush / yr society
          smoked
          EATS EATS
               its terror
                         White Beast
          alive w/ Harpoons
inside it the bones
of whole nations

Slavery, Concentration
Camps, Plantations
Gas Chambers

The death of Reconstruction was
     the death of the dream
     the death of the reality
     The death of any wd be American
               Democracy!

Bloodless "Jaws" whale shark monster
it kills include cultures
now post McCarthy where
is Grapes of Wrath or I Was

A Fugitive or the truth
of itself? Was Sam Spade
a Communist Sympa
thizer? Or Philip Marlowe?
But even that individual cry
for straight shot Democracy
cd finally find itself banned in darkness
while Robotic Horror pornography makes us
consumers of masturbation and degenerating
 values.
       An america where the only academy awards
       go to Ronald Reagan w/ Clarence Pendleton as
       Ben Vereen. "Boogity Boogity" an
       Ellison description of Ellison describing.
       The teeth of imperialism is a chant
       for the dying things needing to die.
       Its poison swelling EAT EAT
       Its cry of terror!

You see (a whispered
      aside)
    even its "humanity"
    (a people of slave holders)
    was a kind
    of minstrelsy

    An unconvincing
    Black Face Act.

Now the flicks are a form of Commerce
          less and less
              of art
    Film innovation was revolutionary
Eisenstein's Red Montage
    With that connection, the tech
nology & casual populist dream

    Equality.
    So much popcorn.
The Jews, Italians, Irish, Poles, & c.
    had first to give up
    being that
to enlarge the baby slave holder
    Fat banker fish
to be its evolved "revolutionary"
    Sleek sea thing
        (Sleek?
    A nigger
    in its teeth
The feed of bulging monsters
so creative they invented
fascism in the black belt
of democracy
So the Black Face, Dixie Land, thin rag, non-"race,"
          Funny hat, Paul Whiteman
          stiff seat, noun baked non swing
          of the "cool," bebop's cover.
          Or for the Shorties & Rodgers
          & Bru's & Becks & the green
          of our dollar - oh man- to
          the "progressive jazz" of glass
          adjectives w/ no where to blow.

Until we get fusion & its con
a cool out of new blues
           turns a chain to a flexible
           rubber unbreakable straw
           for yr elevator colored nouveau,

           to the gallows garden
           of the floating compradors

           where their eggs, like body snatcher
           pods lay hatching way in the middle
           of the air.

           This bend of class
           to the death of itself
           & rebirth in fake neon flames.
Elvis Presley was the FDR of
           the 1950's, the philosophy
           was workable & when the
           Beatles moved in simply slander
           them w/belittling Jesus
           & enlarge the American market.
           Nigger Music became figure
           music. Chocolate death
           Plastic. Instead of rejection-
The Huge monster's mouth
Him/Her's protein digesting skin

           To Europe? To The Past?
           But leave reality to the
             real & the living

By the end of the 19th century

they cd convert the sorrow songs
to Barber Shop
Quartets.

"There was Something I Wanted to Tell You." (33) Why?

African Lullaby
Babenzele Pygmies,
S. Africa

Revolutionary War
 gamed
     sold
        out
           The Tories
still in control
of the culture

English Departments
still
& the money & "culture"
in an "English"
accent.

The Green Mtn Boys
Tom Paine The Bill
of Rights

tried to cut
it

    But then 19th century
    Explosion, Free the
    Slaves, Kill feudal

ism, Give rights
to the Farmer & Worker

the vote to Women

But that got blew
    Hayes-Tilden, Bloody
         Democrats

      Traitor
      Republicans

The Ku Klux Klan
(A murder Gang!)

& that leap, into industrial society
democracy they sd
Got all but Killed
    tho murdered
    many times!

Marx, Engels, Lenin, Stalin, Mao, Ho
    Fidel, Nkrumah
    Martin, Sandino
    & Malcolm X

Have all been
betrayed

All revolutions bear their own
betrayal, & betrayers
The world is complex

its reality materially
simple

It is the dying of the life

the quenching of the spark
the greying of the light
the cold whiteness of the recently
full of flaming inspired intelligent
heart! The dead entrail of our
      collective traditional
      enemy. Animal
      connections. Metaphysics.
      Greed. Anti Science
      lives. Ugly in power
      and uglying up our only
      life.

The rot, the lie, the opposite
will always, if there is ever
that, exist. As life means death
and hot cold. Darkness lights'
closest companion. Its twisted,
      & rises as a spiral. It is No &
Yes, and not It for long.

      Motion, the beat, tender mind
you humans even made music.
      But, our memory anywhere
as humans and beyond, parallel
to everything, is rise is new is
Changed, a glowing peaceful
Musical
World.

What betrays revolution is the need
for revolution. It can not stop in life.
Whoever seeks to freeze the moment is

instantly, & for that instant, *mad!*

We are servants of life in upward
progressive motion. Fanners
of the flame. Resistance is Electric.
Fred sd, its measurable on every
block.

The wd be stoppers of revolution
are its fossil fuel

Winter comes
and Spring

We can sometimes
hear
explosions!

YMCA #35

After The Rain
Trane

We talked all the time
    as spirits we were
      allowed.
        & watched the different
        primates in their turns
        & elegant twists

We caught the rising virus
    like a style of neon
    murders. A calm
    blood washing upward

Between giggles & drunk laughter
    wisdom hit the walls
    & ceiling, windows
      closed if open
        opened if
        closed

It was never quiet
    no familiarities
      were permitted

The good guys sat
    & watched the door

the wizards crawled
from 14th St to the
outer crust

Colors & rain
The well dressed well spoken
The poverty stricken
The lonely
The important
maniacs

They were singing through their
noses, & fingers
Everybody was a headline
A massacre that cd not
be a revelated gorilla

These were rich people & Heroes
The stink was not stink, the garbage
not really garbage. If you cd bend concrete
& hang like the high tent of drunken rapists
Applause wd rock & roll you in yr dreams

Awards could be coughs
hands reaching
poetry of climaxes
proposed. Crippled

Weasels I knew
& sang a song
for the airplane
underground

Not to be subjective
   a heart full of dashes
      no opening through backs
         exploding in their
           dreams.

It is not enough to witness, you are
   somewhere anyway
      & you wont sweat.

2

Riding through the valley
   Sundays coldness a hole
      in summer. A red dark ball
     pasted over
       with notes

But picture The Tempts
   Do-walking
      clean among black
     waves

Picture a blinding whiteness
   like Cab Calloway's
     shoes

the nigger computers
   bluely reporting
     ghosts ahead
who are cannibals

We ponder for the Bop-trillionith
    time

    The Madness
      of the Gods

The Turn Around Y36

The Turn Around
Hank Mobley

Jack Johnson

        was convicted
  of White Slavery!
  He was probably
the only person ever
convicted in this
        country
          of Slavery!

              -Coyt's Son

("One More Time")

Humph
T. Sphere Monk

Likewise
in all these years
I only seen one time
Downbeat called somebody
a "racist" from the front cover
& that was LeRoi Jones. Was
the only time.

              -Likewise

Lord Haw Haw (as Pygmy) #37

All Blues
Miles

We were here

        before

   God

   We

      invented

Him.

   Why?

That's a good/ god damn
    question.

Speech
#38 (or Y We say it this way)

Be Bop
Diz

OoBlahDee
Ooolyacoo
Bloomdido
OoBopShabam
Perdido Klackto-
      Veestedene
Salt Peanuts oroonie
     McVouty
       rebop

Ornithology
BaBa Ree Bopp

Ooo Shoobie
    Doobie

& The Sisters
Dooie Blah
&
Dooie Blee

a Kuka mop

Bee Doop Doop
    ie Doo

pie   -Lemon Drop
    Be Doopie
      Doop Dop

  Squirrel
in The Glass
  Enclosure

  of the essential
Transbluesency

We dreamt Paradise
    w/you
    Naima

Savoying
Balue Bolivared

in black Night
Indigo

Brownie Red
Hollywood Hi Noon
    Trane Lights

  Salaam Thunder
     electricity trademark

Yr heart
in Repetition

    de Milos

Monk's Shades
  made the tru/man
  of a Hairy
    Square
   symbol
  in faded corniness

Gold Electric
Natural Grace
    like
        Freedom

 Horns
of our
  Description - Desperatenesses'
        Drums

Sharp spectrum Blace
     painted hard light

Lush life romance
   ancient
      trade.

Hideehideehidee hee
ooooohhhhhhhhhh

  Oh Imperial Ghost
   who is no
    Ghost
    & Real

Autumn

I think of you
& the sorrow
of gates

& absences in your soul
                America
            like the dead

            spaces

        like ignorance

    between the

            stars

The Ape said,
"Floogie,
        Lucy, Baby!"

Human light
    in your
        African
                    Eyes.

    Travelin Travailing
Majestic
            Life Form

        Scatting

Boogieing

Cosmos In

Cosmos

Rhythm

Rapping, capping
        hand
      slapping

Black Poet

Chanting

to the 1st fire.

So the King Sold the Farmer #39

Angels & Demons At Play
Sun Ra

The   Ghost

     Ghost

Watch out

     for the Ghost

     Ghost get you

     Ghost

     Watch out
         for the
     Ghost

In bitter darkness screams sharpness as smells
   & Seas black voice
   Wails
   in the death filled
   darkness

Their bodies disease beneath intoxicated floors
A seas shudder afraid its turned
               to Blood

The bodies
  they will, in death's shill
  to Lionel Hampton
Ghost Look out
    for the Ghost

Ghost
  is have us
 chains
  is be with
   dying

   is caught

Sea mad, maniac
    drunken
  Killing sea

        Ghooooooooost

        Ghooooooooost

The chains
  & dark
  dark &
   dark, if there was "light"
      it meant
        Ghooost

Rotting family we
  ghost ate
    three

A people flattened chained
    bathed & degraded
       in their own hysterical waste

below
beneath
under neath
deep down
up under

       grave cave pit
       lower & deeper
      weeping miles below
           skyscraper gutters

Blue blood hole into which blueness
is the terror, massacre, torture
   & original western
        holocaust

    Slavery

  We were slaves

    Slaves

    Slaves

Slaves

—
Slaves

—
Slaves

–
   We were

Slaves

–
Slaves

–

   They threw
     our lives
     a way

Beneath the violent philosophy
     of primitive
        cannibals

   Primitive
   Violent
   Steam driven
   Cannibals

RR

My Brother

Y The Link Will Not Always Be "Missing"
#40

The Wise One
Trane

Think of Slavery
   as
    Educational!

Select Bibliography

Preface to a Twenty Volume Suicide Note. New York: Totem Press, 1961.
Blues People: Negro Music in White America. New York: William Morrow &
 Co., 1963.
The Dead Lecturer. New York: Grove Press, 1964.
Dutchman and The Slave. New York: Grove Press, 1964.
The System of Dante's Hell. New York: Grove Press, 1965.
Home: Social Essays. New York: William Morrow & Co., 1966.
The Baptism & The Toilet. New York: Grove Press, 1967.
Tales. New York: Grove Press, 1967.
Black Music. New York: William Morrow & Co., 1968.
Four Black Revolutionary Plays. Indianapolis: The Bobbs-Merrill Co., 1969.
Black Magic: Collected Poetry, 1961–1967. Indianapolis: The Bobbs-Merrill
 Co., 1969.
In Our Terribleness. Indianapolis: The Bobbs-Merrill Co., 1970.
It's Nation Time. Chicago: Thirld World Press, 1970.
Jello. Chicago: Thirld World Press, 1970.
Raise Race Rays Raze: Essays Since 1965. New York: Random House, 1971.
Spirit Reach. Newark: Jihad Productions, 1972.
Hard Facts. Newark: Congress of Afrikan People, 1975.
The Motion of History and Other Plays. New York: William Morrow & Co.,
 1976.
Selected Plays and Prose of Amiri Baraka/LeRoi Jones. New York: William
 Morrow & Co., 1979.

Selected Poetry of Amiri Baraka/LeRoi Jones. New York: William Morrow & Co., 1979 (includes *Poetry for the Advanced*).

The Sydney Poet Heroical. New York: I. Red Books, 1979.

AM/TRAK. New York: Phoenix Book Shop, 1979.

reggae or not! New York: Contact II Publications, 1981.

In the Tradition, privately published pamphlet, 1982 (later in *The Music*)

Daggers and Javelins: Essays, 1974–1979. New York: William Morrow & Co., 1984.

The Autobiography of LeRoi Jones/Amiri Baraka. New York: Freundlich Books, 1984.

The Music: Reflections on Jazz and Blues (with Amina Baraka), New York: William Morrow & Co., 1987.

Amiri Baraka/LeRoi Jones Reader. Ed. W.J. Harris. New York: Thunder's Mouth Press, 1991.

5 Bop Trees (with Amina Baraka). Newark: Rising Tide, 1992.

Heathens. Louisville: Heaven Press, 1994.

Why's, Wise, Y's. Chicago: Thirld World Press, 1995.

Amiri Baraka (LeRoi Jones) was born in Newark, New Jersey, in 1934. He attended Rutgers and Howard Universities, leaving the latter in 1954 to enlist in the U.S. Air Force. In 1957 he settled in New York's Greenwich Village and became a central figure in that bohemian scene, collaborating on and coediting several important literary publications, including *Yugen, Floating Bear,* and *Kulchur.* He gained national attention in 1964, with the New York production of his Obie Award-winning play, *Dutchman.* After the death of Malcolm X in 1965, Baraka became a Black Nationalist, moving first to Harlem and then back to Newark. In 1974, he proclaimed his commitment to International Socialism, Third World Marxism, and definitively repudiated Nationalism.

Baraka has produced over twenty plays, three jazz operas, seven non-fiction books, a novel, and some fifteen volumes of poetry. He has been the recipient of grants from both the Rockefeller Foundation and the National Endowment for the Arts, as well as the Langston Hughes Award from the City College of New York. He is currently a professor of Africana Studies at SUNY-Stony Brook. He lives with his wife, the poet Amina Baraka, in Newark.

Paul Vangelisti is an award-winning poet, translator and editor. His latest book, *Nemo,* has just appeared from Sun&Moon Press in Los Angeles. Currently, from that lost city, he edits *Ribot,* the annual report of the College of Neglected Science.

Poet, dramatist, essayist, fiction writer, and political activist, **Amiri Baraka** is considered by many to be one of the most influential and preeminent African-American literary figures of our time. Over the past thirty years, in addition to some thirteen volumes of poetry, he has produced over twenty plays, three jazz operas, seven volumes of nonfiction, and a novel. He has been awarded numerous literary prizes and honors, including an Obie Award for play-writing and the Langston Hughes Award from the City College of New York. He lives, with his wife, the poet Amina Baraka, in his native city of Newark, New Jersey.

Paul Vangelisti is an award-winning poet, translator, and editor. His latest book, *Nemo*, has just appeared from Sun&Moon Press in Los Angeles. From that lost city, he edits *Ribot*, the annual report of the College of Neglected Science.

Printed in the United States
71192LV00005B/53